The Station of No Station

The Station of No Station

Open Secrets of the Sufis

∞∞∞∞∞

Henry Bayman

North Atlantic Books
Berkeley, California

Printed in the United States of America

Published by North Atlantic Books
P.O. Box 12327
Berkeley, California 94712
Distributed to the book trade by Publishers Group West

Cover and book design by Jan Camp

The calligraphy in Arabic on the front cover, by an anonymous Turkish calligrapher, reads: "I bear witness that there is no god but God, and that Mohammed is His servant and Messenger."

The Station of No Station: Open Secrets of the Sufis is sponsored by the Society for the Study of Native Arts and Sciences, a nonprofit educational corporation whose goals are to develop an educational and crosscultural perspective linking various scientific, social, and artistic fields; to nurture a holistic view of the arts, sciences, humanities, and healing; and to publish and distribute literature on the relationship of mind, body, and nature.

North Atlantic Books are available through most bookstores. To contact North Atlantic directly, call 800-337-2665 or visit our website at www.northatlanticbooks.com.

Substantial discounts on bulk quantities of North Atlantic books are available to corporations, professional associations, and other organizations. For details and discount information, contact the special sales department at North Atlantic Books.

Library of Congress Cataloging-in-Publication Data:

Bayman, Henry, 1951–.
    The Station of No Station: Open Secrets of the Sufis / by Henry Bayman.
        p. cm.
    Includes bibliographical references.
    ISBN 1-55643-240-2 (alk. paper)
    1. Sufism. 2. Sufism—Essence, genius, nature. 3. Sufism—Doctrines. I. Title.
    BP189 .B42 2001
    297 .4—dc21

                                                                    CPI

                                                            00-060961

1 2 3 4 5 6 7 8 9 / 05 04 03 02 01

A MAN, IN SEARCH OF TRUTH, IS ON HIS WAY TO KONYA (FAMED FOR ITS MEN OF KNOWLEDGE), WHEN HE MEETS A TRAVELER RETURNING FROM THAT SAME CITY. AFTER GREETING ONE ANOTHER, THE SECOND MAN ASKS THE SEEKER WHAT TAKES HIM THERE.

"I AM LOOKING FOR GOD, AND I BELIEVE THAT THERE ARE PEOPLE THERE WHO CAN HELP ME FIND HIM."

TO WHICH HE REPLIES:

"HOW STRANGE! I SAW HIM YESTERDAY, AND HE WAS LOOKING FOR YOU!"

Contents

Contents

Contents

PREFACE

It's possible that the truth lies in the fashionable direction.
But if it is in another direction, who will find it?
. . . Dare to follow the beat of a different drum.
                                    —RICHARD P. FEYNMAN

∽∽∽∽∽

During the last quarter of the twentieth century, I was in close contact with the Sufi masters of Central Anatolia in Turkey. Most of this period was spent in association with Master (and Mr.) Ahmet Kayhan.

The Islamic Sufism practiced and preached by these masters is so different, so wonderful, and so uplifting that I consider it my duty to humanity to make its existence known. Here is something so valuable that the whole world stands in need of it.

Peter D. Ouspensky suspected that such a source exists, and now stands confirmed. John G. Bennett, in an effort to track down Gurdjieff's[1] teachers, uncovered the lineage's Central Asian precedents just before he died. Even if we do not know them, we must consider ourselves very lucky indeed to live in the same world as these luminaries.

The Master's approach combined the best faces of Islam and Sufism—faces that are actually inseparable from one another. It may come as a surprise to some that this is no recent synthesis, but an integral wisdom passed down from the very beginning via an authentic and authoritative chain of transmission.

The Master spoke of Islam, yet assuredly you have never seen nor heard of such an Islam, nor have I anywhere else except with the Master. The more I thought about it, the more the conclusion was forced upon me that this must be the pristine, primordial Islam as it must have been practiced by the Prophet himself. (I was not alone in this view; everyone who knew the Master shared it.) For this reason, it was the most delicate and rarest of phenomena, a true Tradition in live action, as if it were being revealed anew today. In his case, Islam and Sufism were identical.

The bitter, harsh and vindictive image cast by some so-called "Moslems" is a result of their failure to be informed by this wisdom. Although they may mean well, they have projected a false picture of Islam into other people's minds, precisely because they themselves have fallen victim to ignorance. (Needless to say, this excludes the vast majority of innocent and peaceful Moslems.) That is why everyone, Moslem or otherwise, stands in need of these teachings.

Let me elaborate by way of a simple example. As Hans Koning has noted: "most of us nowadays would rather come upon a wild animal on a lonely road than upon a strange man. We fear the stranger, 'the other': We feel we don't really understand him. . . . Or we may know him only too well and he may hate us for reasons we choose to forget. . . . Our children are inheriting a world of locks and alarms. . . ." [2]

Now contrast this with Robert Kaplan's account of a shantytown called "Golden Mountain" in Ankara, Turkey. Comparing it with the slums of Abidjan in the Ivory Coast, which has been called "the Paris of West Africa," Kaplan concludes: "in Turkey I learned that shantytowns are not all bad.

"Slum quarters in Abidjan terrify and repel the outsider. In

Turkey it is the opposite. The closer I got to Golden Mountain the better it looked, and the safer I felt. I had $1,500 worth of Turkish lira in one pocket and $1,000 in traveler's checks in the other, yet I felt no fear. Golden Mountain was a real neighborhood." A lady inhabitant told him: "Here we fast. Here we are more religious." [3]

Is it only Abidjan that could benefit from the example of Golden Mountain? What about certain parts of New York, or any city, or—for that matter—the whole world? Doesn't this example indicate that poverty is not the only factor operating behind violence or the lack of it? Doesn't it show that money alone cannot buy peace?

Having lived in a culture where you needn't fear an approaching stranger—where you needn't even think about him, except perhaps to say "Hello"—I want everyone in the world to enjoy this bliss, to share it with them. Earlier, this culture didn't even have locks on doors, because robbery was almost unheard-of. While this may sound too good to be true, the fact that people in the past were able to accomplish it means that it is within the realm of human possibility, and therefore an option open to us also—however remote it might seem from our standpoint. But we don't have to be utopian; I'll settle for Golden Mountain.

No amount of locks will deter a determined thief, and the security walls you erect around yourself (or your "gated community") will only increase your sense of mental insecurity and anxiety. It is only when a majority of people agree upon principles that are inherently capable of lending security that we will not only feel, but actually be, secure.

Make no mistake: what hangs in the balance today is not this or that civilization, but *world* civilization. It is our global civilization that is at stake. It is my heartfelt conviction that we must inform that civilization with the life-giving breath, the tolerance, compassion and humaneness of Islamic Sufism, if it is not to disintegrate into anarchy and chaos. The famous writer E. M. Forster used to be called "the custodian of civilization." Today, we must all take it upon ourselves to become custodians of civilization, and stewards of this planet, if we expect to survive in a tolerable world and to bequeath it to our children, and to our children's children. If we fail to do this, we will not *have* our children's children.

This book owes its existence, and I my thanks, to Richard Grossinger. I had previously written two books on the Master's teachings which are available online, *The Meaning of the Four Books* and *Science, Knowledge, and Sufism*. My original essay on Nietzsche is in the second book, and Mr. Grossinger kindly suggested that this essay could be expanded to constitute a book in itself. The result is what you're reading.

Although it draws upon material from its predecessors, this is in effect an entirely new book. Substantial additions have been made, earlier material has been organized differently, and even the Nietzsche essay—which provided the backbone—has undergone significant change. Hence, it is not simply an abridgement of the previous books.

I want to make it clear from the beginning that while I normally resort to footnotes and other customary tools of scholarship, in speaking of Sufism I drop this convention. The reason is that I am writing directly from memory—from the famous Oral Tradition of Sufism which the Master propagated and we were fortunate enough to hear—from Turkish "field notes" I have taken, or from my own studies. In addition, the sources, even if indicated, would mostly be in Turkish, a language inaccessible to the majority of English readers. Only chapter and verse numbers from the Koran are indicated, in the form (chapter-number:verse-number). When I relate a Sufi teaching-story, it is TYPESET DIFFERENTLY in order to indicate its "trademark."

I must confess to having a problem with terminology. The Master always said that he was practicing and teaching "Islam." By this he meant what he had learned from his own Master, the highest and most ideal sense of Islam as embodied by the Prophet, and the greatest names among his followers, down through history. Furthermore, by "Islam" the Master meant *Islamic Sufism*. It has become customary to use the term "Islam" for exoteric doctrine and practice, and to reserve "Sufism" for the esoteric aspect as denoting Islamic mysticism. (There are even those who seek to isolate Sufism from Islam.) *But in the teachings and example of the Master, there was no such division or distinction.* What he lived, what he taught, was a wisdom which combined the best and brightest aspects of the exoteric and the esoteric in a seamless whole. While he valued Sufism in the sense described above, he always said that the esoteric would get nowhere without the exoteric infrastructure to build upon.

The Master had nothing against practitioners of the Divine Law (followers of the exoteric path) or those interested solely in mysticism (followers of the esoteric path). He regarded both, however, as halfway houses that failed to take account of the other side of the coin. In his view and practice, only the synthesis of the two could yield the necessary transformation of inner energies and the consequent transmutation of the human being. If this is true—and the Master was the living example of that truth—it becomes obvious why so many practitioners on either side have failed to achieve their objective.

It is clear from this that the Master was using "Islam" in a special, all-inclusive sense, a sense we are not ordinarily accustomed to understanding by that term. And now, in recent years and decades, we have come to associate all kinds of vile things with it, as if the religion itself were actually teaching these things and therefore to blame for them. The questionable conduct of latter-day Moslems has become reflected upon the religion itself. But as many Moslems themselves admit, the fault lies with Moslems and not with Islam. A case in point is the Taliban—the interested reader is referred to the Appendix, as that treatment is too large and unwieldy to fit into a preface. "Islam" in its true sense has nothing to do with the flood of negative associations that occurs in our minds as soon as we hear the word. Likewise, it has little to do with the notorious names that have claimed to represent it, or with events we have come to blame on it. Nevertheless, we are now saddled with this depreciated sense of "Islam," which evokes an almost "knee-jerk reaction" in people's minds. "Islam" has become a loaded term. But I have no desire either to defend or deal with it in this sense. Furthermore, it becomes quite cumbersome to say "Islamic Sufism" repeatedly.

So here is how I propose to remedy this problem. Let me state it clearly at the outset. I intend to use the term "Sufism," which has remained pristine and unloaded, in place of what the Master meant when he said "Islam." I want to do this as consistently as I am able to. By using "Sufism" in this special sense, I wish to sidestep the problem of disentangling "Islam" from the associations it brings to mind. I feel that the Master's teachings are too wonderful and important for that. We—the author and the reader alike—have better things to do with our time and energy than to get bogged down in long, drawn-out discussions about what "Islam" means and what it doesn't mean.

Don't get me wrong. *When the Master says "Islam" and I say "Sufism," we both mean the same thing, i.e., Islamic Sufism.* It is not the case that he meant only the exoteric sphere and I mean only the esoteric. I am doing this in order to bypass fruitless arguments that are a waste of time, ink, paper, and attention. There are by now many faces of "Islam," and the one I want to talk about is uniquely that practiced by the Master, not the ones we have come to associate with Kaddafi, Khomeini, Saddam, Taliban, etc., etc. When I say "Islam," however, how am I going to convey in the same breath that it is only this ideal sense I intend and not any of the rest? For this reason, I have decided upon this course. I have the inclination neither to explain nor to defend anything that emerges using the name of "Islam" but which I find to be at variance with the "Islam" I have come to know through the Master. (And the same holds for Sufism.)

There is another reason why I feel justified in doing this. This other aspect of "Islam," as practiced and preached by the Master, is so exalted, so uplifting, and so unknown generally that it is practically "esoteric" to us, not only to non-Moslems but quite likely to Moslems as well. It is uncharted territory, undiscovered country. Superficially, it may resemble the more mundane sense. But I hope to be able to show that we are here in the presence of something which goes beyond that and hence for us—Moslems and non-Moslems alike—is "hidden" at the beginning.

In talking about historical personages and events, however, it is difficult to maintain this usage. There, an "Islamic scholar" has to remain an Islamic scholar and a "Sufi" has to remain a Sufi, simply to avoid confusion. While this is still not, for me, a satisfactory solution, I hope this explanation at the outset will have made clear how I will be using terms.

Further, I shall consistently try to use "God," "the Book," and "the Prophet" instead of "Allah," "the Koran," and "Mohammed," respectively. Since we so often stumble over words and sounds, I want the reader to see if the subject matter still seems impenetrable once these substitutions have been made. Prayer (Arabic *salat,* Persian *namaz*) I shall render by "Formal Prayer," as otherwise it is confused with supplication, whereas "remembrance" (*dhikr*) will be rendered by "invocation." Translations from Turkish into English I have done myself. The gender problem in English confronts us as usual. Suffice it to say that when I speak of God as "He," or when I say "man," I am not imputing masculinity, and unless an explicitly male person is involved, the third-person singular always includes "she."

As always, I owe thanks to Tim Thurston and Peter Murphy, whose help and suggestions have proved invaluable—but for them, this book would not be what it is—as well as to all others who have aided in bringing the book to its present form. My gratitude also to what I call the "Web Library"—all the sources available on the World Wide Web, whether I have used them or not.

I have used more sources than are indicated in the text, but any attempt to give them all would hopelessly swamp us in a tyranny of footnotes. Hence, only those sources that I consider the most germane are indicated. For example, I have not bothered to document what I deem to be more commonly known facts.

To err is human, and there are few books entirely free of errors. If, in spite of all the painstaking care I have taken, any errors do crop up, I plead the reader's indulgence.

Prologue

I

The Background of It All

Monsieur de Fortgibu has nothing on me. Never heard of him? Well, he figures in a Jungian case of synchronicity, a true story related by the French astronomer Camille Flammarion: when M. Deschamps was a little boy in Orleans, he was treated to some plum pudding by a neighbor, M. de Fortgibu. Ten years later, he again encountered plum pudding in a restaurant in Paris. He wanted to order some, but the waiter told him that another customer had already ordered the last remaining dish. M. Deschamps looked; it was M. de Fortgibu who had ordered the dish.

Years later, M. Deschamps was again offered some plum pudding at a gathering. As he ate, he recalled the earlier incidents and told his listeners that the only thing missing at that moment was M. de Fortgibu. Suddenly the door burst open, and a very old man verging on senility staggered in. Who should it be but M. de Fortgibu, who had got hold of the wrong address and come to the party by mistake.

Such "meaningful coincidences"—and I could tell you many more—give us an intimation of the subtler workings of the universe. Behind the coarse mechanics that strike the undiscerning eye, there are connections as fine as the thread of a spider's web, or even finer, justifying Wordsworth's "sense of something far more deeply interfused. . . ." Some people call it "fate," others call it "coincidence." I say names are unimportant; it's the phenomenon and what it portends that count. Such phenomena are too small and slippery to be caught in the coarse meshes of science's net,[4] though they didn't escape the net of the French astronomer. In any case, my discovery of the Master was as fortuitous—or was it?—as M. de Fortgibu and his plum puddings.

Did it all begin there, at the Library of Congress, the repository of all the knowledge in the world? Who knows? I had asked for a book, and the librarians had been unable to locate it. I insisted that it had to be there—how couldn't it? So, although it's against the rules, I was for once allowed to go in and check, to see for myself.

Down and down went the elevator—how much below ground level, I'm unable to say. There were many underground floors like the one I was about to see. Then the doors opened, and all of a sudden I found myself in a hall as large as a football field. To my right and left stretched corridors of shelves as far as the eye could see; and ahead of me, countless such corridors stretching down to the horizon branched off right and left. I entered a corridor on my right; the shelves, piled up to the rafters with books, looked like the Grand Gallery in the Great Pyramid of Cheops. It was the closest thing to the Akashic Records on Earth, and I was overawed. I reached out for a book; the one that arrived in my hands was *The Morning of the Magicians,* by L. Pauwels and J. Bergier, which fell open where the binding was cracked. There I saw an excerpt from Gustav Meyrink's *The Green Face.* The Green Face, I was to find out years later, was—surprise, surprise—none other than Khidr (which means "the green one"). So was it that "Khidr manifestation"—the manifestation of the saving power of Khidr, who helps those in distress—that saved me? And how had Meyrink found out about

Khidr in the alchemistic bookshops tucked away in the narrow back streets of old Prague? I don't know. Anyhow, I began to read:

> You must climb from one rung to another if you want to conquer death.
>
> The lowest rung is called: genius.
>
> What are we to call the higher ones? They are hidden from the mass of mankind and looked upon as legends.
>
> The story of Troy was thought to be a legend until one day a Man had the courage to start excavating by himself.

That is, of course, the story of Heinrich Schliemann, who dreamt as a seven-year-old boy of discovering Homer's fabulous city, and 39 years later actually discovered it, treasure and all. Was he working in vain when, with watch in one hand and Homer in the other, he re-enacted the movements of the Trojan War, retracing the steps of the soldiers? Not at all. A day before the diggings were terminated in 1873, he found one of the most priceless treasures ever from beneath *seven layers* of ancient cities.[5] And today I ask, are believers working in vain when they retrace the movements of a prophet and circumambulate a Holy Sanctuary seven times?

Two other episodes seem relevant: when I was whisked to the top of the Empire State Building by high-speed elevators and beheld the magnificent splendor of New York by night—an ocean of light—and when I visited Cape Canaveral from which the moon rockets were launched, did these have anything to do with my initial descent into the cellars of the Library—an ocean of knowledge? You tell me. Karl Jaspers believed that the universe is a vast cyphertext, a cryptogram, a book of symbols. Over the years I've come to believe (or was it always a deep-seated intuition?) that the universe—and the Koran which is its mirror image—is, to quote Jorge Luis Borges, "an immense liturgical text where the iotas and dots are worth no less than the entire verses or chapters, but the importance of one and the other is indeterminable and profoundly hidden." A work dictated by God is, says Borges, "an absolute text: in other words, a text in which the collaboration of chance [is] calculable as zero . . . nothing can be contingent in the work of an infinite mind."[6] Is this what synchronistic events are trying to help us discover?

In any case, like another Borges character, I too arrived at a mysterious conclusion. The truth, beauty, and goodness you see in anyone are a reflection of a friend, or a Friend of the Friend: "some place in the world there is a man from whom this clarity emanates; some place in the world there is a man who is this clarity," this perfection. Exactly like Borges' inquisitive student, I found a telltale trail to lead me through increasing heights "of reason, of the imagination and of good."[7] As I came closer to the Source, I began to hear rumors. It was said that the Master lived on top of the tallest building in the world; that he lived on top of the world; that *he himself* was the tallest building in the world; that his apartment was the Noah's Ark of our day. At two steps' remove from the Master, I encountered an immensely happy and courteous man; at a remove of one step, I encountered a saint.

Then, one day, I was led into an apartment where an immense spiritual radiance shone from behind a curtain. I caught a reflection of the Master in a glass, a venerable and—to all outward appearances—an ordinary-looking man. So as not to disturb the crowd already there, I sank into an empty chair and began to listen. What follows is, after many years, a report of my discoveries.

But first: who was he? What kind of phenomenon had I encountered?

II
The Flawless Human Being

An Impossible Task

How shall I begin to tell the story of a man who literally defies description? If there is one thing all the thousands of people—from the most diverse backgrounds—who have been graced with his presence would probably agree upon, it is that the Master ("Effendi," in Turkish) is indescribable. I have consulted some friends who knew him, and they all shook their heads sadly, knowing that the attempt was impossible.

The reason is that all language presupposes a common base of human experience. Suppose I tell you, for instance, that I have drunk the juice of a South American fruit, *guanabana*. If you have drunk it too, you will immediately know what I am talking about. But suppose you haven't, and I'm trying to describe it to you. "It's sweet," I say. Now that's nice, it gives you something to work on. But cookies are sweet too, and so is candy. "Its color and texture resemble those of milk," I next add. That gives you some further clues. And I can keep on elaborating details until you have a pretty good approximate idea of what *guanabana* tastes like. But unless you have actually tasted it, you will never really know what I'm talking about.

And the same thing goes with Effendi. The reason is that he was unique—one of a kind, even among Sufi masters—and so, incomparable. Having rushed in where angels fear to tread, I find myself saddled with the thankless job of describing him to a world scarcely equipped with the tools necessary for an adequate comprehension of such a person. Many will say my description is too good to be true, and with them I sympathize entirely—in their shoes, not having seen what we all saw, I too would have found such an account unbelievable.

The task that stands before me, then, is to assume the role of a Fair Witness (as described in Robert Heinlein's *Stranger in a Strange Land:* "The house looks yellow on this side") and submit my account as truthfully and sincerely as I know how. To those who disbelieve, let me say in advance that I don't blame them one bit. The trouble is that this account comes to your doorstep just a bit too late, for it was not so long ago that we watched helplessly as his life, like water, slowly but surely trickled away through our fingers. The only way to verify my story would have been to come and see for yourself. Now that the only sure-fire means of verification is no longer in our hands, people will be entirely justified in their skepticism.

The question might also arise as to how reliable, how objective and impartial, a humble and devoted student of the Master may be, a person who has known him for two decades, and has been able to observe him at close quarters for fifteen years. The answer is: more reliable than you might think. For it is not only a privilege for me to write about the Master; it is also a duty, and this duty can brook no untruth. The slightest deviation from the truth—the slightest misrepresentation—in explaining such a person to the world at large would, to my mind, be fraught with dire consequences. I shall do my best to abide by the ideal of a fair witness, and with the help of God I hope to be as successful as I am humanly able to. But do not forget: what I am going to tell you is an almost illegible replica of the truth, watered down, as it were, to the concentration levels of a homeopathic solution. I doubt that the scarcely discernible traces on this paper will give you much more than the barest inkling of that staggering reality. And I fully accept in advance that the failure to communicate is my shortcoming, not yours.

Perhaps, in the future, others who have known the Master

will come forth to tell their respective stories. Until then, this account will have to suffice as an introduction to the man—pardon me, the Man—and his teachings.

A Hidden Master—In this Day and Age?

The question immediately arises: if a person such as I claim really existed, how is it possible that he remained hidden from public knowledge until his death? How, in this age of instant communications and the Internet, was he able to remain obscure? We have immediate knowledge of a previously undiscovered tribe of primitives in Indonesia; how can a person of such stature manage to avoid detection so completely to the end of his life?

The answer is that this is possible if the person in question shuns the limelight, and if those who know him consider him so precious, and know him to be so indescribable, that they clam up whenever prying eyes rove by. It can happen if his devotees respect their Master's aversion to exposure so much that he remains free to cultivate his garden—themselves—in peace. And it can happen if they consider everything connected with him as a different reality, an enchanted realm that is simultaneously in this world and out of it.

The humility of Grandpa (as those who loved him called him—other epithets were "Father," "Father Ahmet," or "Grandpa Kayhan") is the reason why he did not like to advertise himself. I've been told, for example, that in 1982 he was visited by a Canadian journalist who was so impressed by what he saw that he said to the Master: "Let me publicize you. To the Jews, let me go and say: 'If you're looking for Moses, here he is.' To the Christians, let me pronounce: 'I've discovered Jesus.' And to the Moslems let me say, 'Here is Mohammed.'" The Master refused, and the journalist respected him enough to comply with his wish to remain unexposed. He could have become world-famous, had he so wished.

Also, Turkey is a country that has undeservedly remained obscure to the outside world. Despite the fact that it is a staunch ally of the United States, there are people who wouldn't be able to locate this country on a world map. And the Master hasn't remained entirely unknown. Brief references to him have appeared in the Turkish press, whether veiled or naming him by name. Further, there are Americans, Britons, and people of other nationalities who have gained his acquaintance.

Many are the gurus and enlightened masters, of whatever religion, who ceaselessly labor to make the world a better place to live in, and to them all I extend my best wishes—may they see the fruits of their efforts. Many of them are in the public eye. It appears, however, that the greatest masters always remain hidden from view, and are deciphered only after they pass away.

Who Was He?

So, what kind of person was Effendi (pronounced exactly like the letters F-N-D in English)? This is the hurdle I feared. Well, here goes:

Up to this day, you have met many human beings. Some of them have struck you as having exceptional qualities. Some are more intelligent, some more compassionate, some stronger in moral fiber than others. Some people excel in courage, others in honesty—and so on.

Now, bring together all the admirable traits you have ever seen in any human being. Next, multiply the sum by a thousandfold. That, approximately, will give you what people lovingly referred to as "Effendi."

This is exactly the point where incredulity, and consequently my predicament, are bound to set in. But this is also the point on which I must remain adamant. The Master cannot be described in any terms, except by superlatives.

I can well understand the consternation of the disciples of Jesus in their attempts to describe him to others. The same goes for the followers of the Buddha or the companions of Mohammed. One has to be faced with a difficulty of a similar order to comprehend what they were trying to cope with.

The problem is compounded when you find out that the Master was basically unschooled. He learned to read and write only during his military service, in his twenties. But that has to be set against the fact that he was trained by the greatest Master of them all: Hadji ("Pilgrim") Ahmet Kaya Effendi, his own master, who was called "Keko" (Kurdish for "Father") by his followers.

But what about the warts, the feet of clay? The short answer is: there were no warts. And I am not concealing anything here. All right, the Master, being human, was prone to the afflictions of humanity. He was sick most of the time in his old age, and suffered from a badly healed broken leg and failing eyesight in his final years. But this is not what we usually consider to be warts, blemishes of the human personality. In all those fifteen years, I saw him really angry only once, and his only response was the softly spoken word, "Quiet." Those are the "worst-case characteristics."

A Visit to Effendi

Suppose, then, that you had the good fortune to meet the Master face to face, and I or someone else had elected to take you there. What would you have encountered?

We would have approached a four-story apartment building on a major road in Ankara, climbed the stairs to the top floor, and rung the bell of one of the apartments. We would have been ushered in by a person opening the door and led into a large living room. In no time at all, if he wasn't resting or otherwise occupied, you would have had the audience of the Master. Of all gurus and masters, he was the most accessible.

You would find yourself in the presence of a gracious old gentleman. He was a lean person—he once told me he never weighed more than 55 kilograms—perhaps six feet tall, but stooped in his old age. Despite his great age, his graying hair and beard, which were originally black, made him appear no more than 65 or 70.

Even if you were an ant, he would treat you like a king. Pleasantries would be exchanged over a cup of tea. Whether or not you had arrived in the middle of a serious discussion with other people present, you would slowly realize a peculiar sensation—as if all your troubles and sorrows were ebbing away, and you were being filled with a quiet joy. If you were psychically sensitive, you might also feel a tingling in the middle of your forehead. And, regardless of whether you had only engaged in small talk, you would leave the apartment with a great feeling of elation. And this would continue to occur each time you visited him. Many were those who dropped in for five minutes to investigate, and stayed a lifetime.

If you continued your visits, you would have come to the conclusion that the Master had the uncanny ability to read minds. This was alarming to some; others took it for granted. The Master never laid claim to such an ability, of course, and he was always discreet in such matters. But suppose you went to visit him with a specific question in mind. And suppose others were present, so that you weren't able to voice your question. As he talked, you would by and by realize that he was answering your question without even speaking to you.

It goes deeper. People have told me that on some occasion when they were alone together, Effendi told them the innermost secrets of their lives, memories never disclosed to anyone and known only to themselves.

And deeper. A British friend visited him one day. The Master was unavailable, my friend intended to go to a seaside resort on the Aegean coast, and while he was waiting for the Master, he kept repeating over and over in his head the Turkish phrase for "Should I go?" which he had just learned. As he was pondering this thought, the housemaid came in and, for no apparent reason, turned on the TV set. There, on the screen, my friend saw the fleeting words: "Go, you can go" in Turkish—a fortuitous display from whatever TV channel the set happened to be tuned to at that moment. The maid turned off the TV set, again for no apparent reason, and left the room. Coincidence? You tell me.

A sage cannot be known from his external appearance. Many people who came could not see beyond his hair and his beard—at first. Later, as they became better acquainted, they would begin to understand something of Effendi.

If you continued your visits, you would learn many things you had never known before. And finally, you would come to realize that here was the most lovable, the most adorable, absolutely the most wonderful person on Earth.

His Life

The bare bones of the Master's biography are quickly told. The closest I can make out is that he was born in late winter or early spring, 1898. Since he died on August 3, 1998, he was a hundred years and seven months old when he passed away.

On his ID papers, his birthdate is given as 1903 (1321, reckoned by the lunar calendar, which was then in use). Because vital statistics were not conscientiously collected in those years, however, he was registered together with his half-brother when the latter was born several years after him. His birthplace was the small village of Mako (Aktarlar, as it is now known) near Poturge in the province of Malatya.

He lost his father when he was only a year old. His mother

remarried, but died when he was seven. After that, he stayed with an aunt for a while. Even at an early age, stories are told that indicate he was brave and under divine protection, perhaps supporting the claim that sages are born and not made. (They're both born *and* made, actually; we can't neglect either face of the nature/nurture coin.) He was only four or five years old when he first met, and was extremely impressed by, his Master (Keko).

When the last Sultan departed from Istanbul on a ship (November 17, 1922), he was there by chance to witness the occasion. From then on, he would shuttle often between the large cities of Istanbul in the west or Ankara in Central Anatolia and Malatya in the east, for it was in the village called Ali Bey near Tillo (in Malatya) that Keko resided.

Ahmet Kayhan settled in Ankara in the 1930s and married Hajar (March 25, 1937), who remained his wife until his death. Keko passed away on May 7, 1944. He was a very great master, routinely visited by hundreds of people, and when he died the task of enlightening the people fell to Musa Kiazim, who had been Keko's fellow-disciple during and after the First World War. With the death of Kiazim Effendi in 1966, Grandpa Kayhan "donned the Mantle."

Up to this time he had taken odd jobs in Ankara, opened three shops, finally settling down as a government employee at the State Waterworks, from which he retired for reasons of health. All this he did in order to support his family. He had four children, two girls and two boys, from Mother Hajar. They, in turn, have lived to see their grandchildren.

From the sixties onward, Grandpa conducted the activity of enlightening the people. Since he was retired, he was able to devote his full time to this effort. I once counted 47 visitors on an average day, but in recent years this number increased substantially as more people came to know him.

The facts of a Sufi saint's life, however, rarely tell us much about who he was. I have related the above only because it is necessary, not because it is helpful for an appreciation of Effendi.

His Line of Descent

Master Kayhan's chain of transmission is traced through the Prophet, his close associate and first Caliph Abu Bakr, Abdulqader Geylani, Bahauddin Naqshband, Ahmed Sirhindi, Abdullah Dehlewi, Khalid Baghdadi, Sheikh Samini, Osman Badruddin, and Ahmet Kaya Effendi. I have omitted most of the names in the Golden Chain from the list and concentrated only on the most illustrious.

It is said that the line of Prophethood started as a light in the forehead of Adam. Down through the ages this light was transferred from the forehead of one prophet to another, until it reached Mohammed, the last prophet. Mohammed combined the attributes of Prophethood and Sainthood within himself.

Now although prophethood had come to an end, the light of sainthood again continued down through the ages, passing from one great master to another. It emerged from Mecca with the Prophet, passed on to Baghdad with Sheikh Geylani (founder of the Qadiri Order), traveled to Bokhara in Central Asia and devolved on Shah Naqshband (founder of the Naqshbandi Order), went south to India with Imam Rabbani (Sirhindi) and Abdullah of Delhi (later to be known as New Delhi), returned to Baghdad with Maulana Khalid, finally traveling north to find itself in Eastern Anatolia. This circuit of the light of sainthood continued for hundreds of years, and will be completed only at the end of time—so it is said.

The Sufi Orders are, in Effendi's words, "spiritual schools"— a fact recognized by Peter Ouspensky. Of course, the fact that the Saintlight moves on doesn't mean that its former abode is left neglected. The Naqshbandi (Naqshi for short) Order's spiritual schools and training continued after the departure of the Saintlight. It was to the tail end of these that George I. Gurdjieff latched on towards the end of the nineteenth century, and many of the unique elements in his teachings are imported direct from the Central Asian Sufi schools. John G. Bennett, a student of Gurdjieff, traced the migration of the schools to Turkey, but died on the verge of discovering the precise whereabouts of the Saintlight.

The long and short of it is, the Master was squarely at the center of the highest expression of traditional Islamic Sufism, in the line of the Samini Branch of the Naqshbandi Order. Yet at the same time, there was no one more modern or more open-minded than he. (I must again stress that this is not simply my personal opinion. Rather, I am quoting from a follower, this time a modern-minded lady.)

Although this was Grandpa's spiritual pedigree, yet he was beyond all orders, sects, or schools. And though he was a devout Moslem, he embraced people of all religions.

How I Met Him

The circumstances of my life conspired to bring me in contact with the Master in early spring, 1978. (I still kick myself for not having written down the precise date, but it was probably early March.) By then, I had been undergoing Sufi training with a master for three years, and it was he who took me to Effendi. We entered his presence together. There are nonverbal ways in which Sufi masters convey what they want to people, and within a few moments I became aware that I was in the presence of an exceptional human being. (This is not intended to imply any great legerdemain on my part, for the Master could introduce himself to anyone with equal ease.)

After 1980, I attended the Master's discussion groups more

frequently. From May 1983 onward, excluding normal working hours or vacations, I had the incredible good fortune to be almost continually in the presence of the Master until his death.

The Views of Others

I could draw on many accounts from eyewitnesses, and perhaps in the future I shall do so. For now, however, I have confined myself to the following excerpts.

An American friend who is attached to another Sufi master: "Ahmed Effendi is certainly unique and special, but it is a uniqueness which has nothing foreign about it and nothing that separates. . . . For me it is a quality which I can only call intimacy. I do not know any other more respectful term for the quality. What I mean is the degree to which Effendi seems to be within one's own self, one's own being, and the complete ease and directness of his communication, literally transcending speech and language and culture and time and history, while at the same time establishing, confirming and justifying them . . . there was never a need to speak, and my increasing knowledge of Turkish, which did add immeasurably to the relish of conversation with Effendi, never seemed to increase the intimacy of the presence of Effendi in my heart, or the hearts of any of my friends who love him. . . . Although I am upset [by his departure] . . . I feel a deep and profound joy and happiness in knowing that I can not be separated from his love in any way whatsoever."

A British friend: "One visit I made to Effendi symbolizes something I think is essential to what I experienced each and every time I was lucky enough to be in his presence. A lady arrived to that amazing house where the door was always open (except for those rare occasions where his health precluded any conversation) and where the Turkish custom of taking off your shoes took on a new dimension of meaning. She was greeted with

the customary courtesy, served tea, and asked how she was. At
this she said, 'Dear Effendi, when I come into your presence I feel
as if all of my cares and troubles have been lifted from me and left
at your door!' He smiled (that indescribably beautiful smile that
seemed to light the whole room!) and said affectionately, knowing full well that she had voiced what the majority of the people
in that crowded apartment on a busy Saturday morning were
experiencing, 'Yes, you are right, my dear, but how much better it
would have been if you had left your self at the door.'

"Utter selflessness. Had I not witnessed it I would be unable
to comprehend it. And for literally thousands of people he did
the same: beckoning them to step through that door into that
space of the purest light and grace."

A Turkish newspaper columnist: "Where he lived was, for us,
like a place where the sun never set. We would go there whenever we were down or blue. We would return to our dark world
with feelings of great peace, as if bathed inside and outside in
fountains of light. . . .

"Was he Qadiri? Was he Naqshi? I don't know. I never asked
his disciples. Nor did I find it necessary. What difference does it
make what Order's Sheikh he was? Without a doubt, he was a
great saint of God. His door was open to everyone. Like Rumi,
he embraced all sinners."[8]

The Master's Teachings

Hadji Ahmet Kayhan (for he, too, performed the Pilgrimage to
Mecca, or *Hajj*) was a Man of Knowledge, or a Man of Wisdom.
With him there was no distinction between Buddhist, Jew,
Christian, or Moslem. He was far beyond drawing distinctions
in the ordinary manner. For him there were only human beings,
and to all he counseled the same teaching: God exists, and God
is One. Abide by the Divine Law. Work for the establishment

of peace on Earth, love one another, and devote yourself to serving your fellow-(wo)men. Feel compassion for all creatures, for even a fly.

As you can see, his teachings were independent of time, space, or geography, and so, truly universal. His pamphlets on world peace aroused favorable responses from a former French president, from the Pope, and from both the then-president and prime minister of Israel. If he had survived longer, his intention would have been to continue to call men to peace on Earth. He was against all weapons of mass destruction, because these are against all forms of life.

One of his followers described to me what he had personally understood from the Master's teachings. "Law and justice exist," he said, "because of conscience, and conscience exists because of love. If you love someone, you cannot violate that person's rights. And that's what the Divine Law is all about. It gives you the guidelines of how to behave as you would if you loved that person. I have seen no one else," he added, "who preaches this fundamental fact." I relate this because it reflects an average perception of what the Master taught.

But this was only the beginning. The Master's curriculum included everything in the spiritual field from kindergarten to university.

Methodology

The methods of the Master in teaching his students varied, yet there were discernible trends. He would not tax a pupil beyond his or her capacity. In accordance with the saying of the Prophet, he would speak to the level of understanding of his listeners. He had the knack of explaining the most complicated things in the simplest terms. If, despite this, the person didn't understand, he would repeat what he said. He would keep at it until the listener understood, and once he saw he had communicated his message successfully, he would say no more about it. From then on, it was the listener's responsibility to heed the contents of the message.

The Master was an inexhaustible repository of Sufi teaching-stories and anecdotes. He would select the most appropriate to a given occasion, sometimes relating events from his life history. He had infinite love and respect for his own Master and would sometimes fondly relate a memory of the times they had together.

What was outstanding about the Master's use of teaching-stories, however, was his ability to string them together in the appropriate order to achieve exactly the desired result. In this respect, he had the virtuosity of a composer with them.

He would quickly discover the *forte*—the strongest virtue—of a person. He once told me that only a moment was enough for a true *murshid* (Islamic guru) to take the snapshot of a person—I'm inclined to call it a kind of spiritual X-ray. He would then cultivate that virtue of the person, also supplementing this with whatever "vitamins" were deficient in a student's constitution.

When a question was asked of him, he always answered it, even if he appeared to refuse at first. If something was insisted upon despite what he said, he might appear to give in, but it was always what he first said that counted.

At times, he left his students without explicit guidance. It might be surmised that some activity, some energetic effort, was expected of them during such periods.

The analogy has been suggested to me that the Master was giving each one of us a handful of seeds. It was our duty to plant these seeds, cultivate them, and see them through to maturity and the bearing of fruit. Another analogy is that he was giving us keys to unlock the secret chambers of our brains. We all know that a human being utilizes, say, two or three percent of the capacity of his brain. Suppose an Einstein uses ten percent. What, then, are we to call those who utilize 50 percent, 75 percent?

What are we to call a person who utilizes it to the full? *That* question is left as an exercise for the reader.

Formal Organization

The Master had no formal organization to speak of. Although he was in the Naqshbandi line of descent, there were no dervish convents (*takkas*), no ceremonies, no special rituals, and no formalities. The convents were disbanded in 1928 by the newly-formed Turkish Republic, but with the Master I learned that there was no need for them. True spirituality could be exercised and conveyed without any formal structure at all—all that is necessary is acceptance on the part of the teacher, and devotion, sincerity, and effort on the part of the student. Having served their purpose, the *takkas* had passed into history as defunct sociological institutions.

Instead there were *ad hoc* discussion groups, which came into existence on the spur of the moment with whomever might be present at that time. Visiting the Master and participating in these discussions were very important. A leaflet or pamphlet distributed by the Master might be read, which he might interrupt at any time in order to clarify or emphasize a certain point. Even this might not be necessary, as the *baraka* (spiritual action or power) of the Master could work in total silence. When one's spiritual "battery" was "discharged," one could go back to the Master for a "recharge." If love can be defined as "giving without receiving—or asking for—anything in return," then the Master loved his following. They, in turn, tried to love him, but generally failed in this task.

A group could include people from widely diverse backgrounds, and the Master would find their lowest common denominator. In addressing one, he would address all. When everyone left, that was the end of that group.

The Mystery of Effendi

If one spent sufficient time with the Master, one might have come to the conclusion that he possessed a closely guarded secret.

Some of the things he said and did were eminently logical and reasonable. Other things would be impervious to comprehension, no matter how hard one exerted oneself. Some of the things he said would become comprehensible much later, as events took their course. It could take years before you were able to decipher them. As historian Paul Johnson has noted of Jesus' utterances in a similar context, the Master was a complicated man and sometimes spoke in a complicated way. One of his granddaughters, who had been with her grandparents almost from her birth, once told me that it was hard to figure out what made him tick. I don't believe anyone ever figured him out. Whatever this secret was, it went with him to the grave.

The phenomenon of the Master has prompted me to think that Jesus had a similar mystery to him, and this caused his followers to misinterpret what they saw as the Deity. Furthermore, I'm thinking that the Buddha might also have shared this mystery, due to which reason he presented it under the terms of *nirvana* (extinction) and *sunyata* (void). It was to avoid a situation similar to that of Jesus, perhaps, that he did not mention God. This is only my own personal opinion, of course, and has nothing to do with the teachings of the Master.

Whatever this mystery was, it gave the Master a charm. Of all human beings, he was the most charming. He attracted people as a magnet attracts iron filings. People found him irresistible, and the more everyone saw of him, the more they wanted to see. The reason was not curiosity. Once you have seen the truly wondrous phenomenon of a fully realized human being, the respect and love you feel for him or her cause you to return again and again. Oh, I know the old adage: "Believe only half of what you see, and none of what you hear," but half of what I saw—a quarter, a hundredth of what I saw!—was already tremendous enough. And don't say here I go exaggerating again, because I'm not.

What inspired love in the thousands of people who knew him? What caused university professors to be the humble students of this unschooled man? He was not rich, so the reason was not economic. He was not a politician, so the reason was not political. Yet he knew things no one else knew, saw things no one else saw. This, however, is still not sufficient to explain the irresistible attraction this hundred-year-old man had on all those people.

Perhaps his secret was Love.

Ask any of his followers, and they would have answered: "He loves *me*." Ask any other, and they would have given the same reply. He treated everyone without exception, whether the highest or the lowliest, the blameworthy no less than the admirable, as if they were kings. He was deeply courteous towards everyone: here, "courtesy" means noble behavior, stemming from nobility of spirit. Everyone can love what seems lovable to him, but to embrace the unlovable with equal ease bespeaks a love that is unbounded, a love that is limitless. Deep down, many of us harbor thoughts that are never expressed. To be able to love anyone, *in full cognizance of those inner thoughts and feelings*, is, I submit, the feat of no ordinary human being. He showered each one, no matter how unworthy, with that universal love, the kind of love we usually associate with Christ. And because he loved everyone, everyone, in return, loved him.

His people were an interesting lot. Some might have been inclined to view them as a herd, as an uncritical, imperceptive bunch of simpletons. As I got to know them better, I discovered that each had an exceptional ability—or even several—and they might not even know it. These virtues the Master unfailingly discerned and cultivated.

The Perfect Man

The existence of a person like Ahmet Kayhan forced those who knew him to reconsider and redefine what it means to be human. Just as a single white elephant is enough to prove that not all elephants are gray, the existence of a human being like Effendi forces us to stop the presses and rewrite the books.

All these years, we've been talking about human potentials and possibilities. But what are they, really? What are their limits?

Suppose someone you don't know came up to you and said: "I have met the Superman, and he is Mohammed. In their time, Jesus and the Buddha were the supermen of their ages." It's the twenty-first century, and he's saying that. What would you think? And what would you say?

Having met the Master, I don't wonder that his disciples confused Jesus with God or the Son of God. No man can be God, of course, and yet I can well understand their difficulty in groping for a label. What is amazing is that someone like the Master, who should ordinarily belong to the Age of the Prophets, could be found and encountered in the second half of the twentieth century.

In order to describe the phenomenon of the total spiritual transmutation of a human being, the Sufis have developed the concept of the Perfect Human (*al-insan al-kamil*). One could also use the Nietzschean concept of the Superman, or the Chinese concept of the superior man or true man. I hasten to add, however, that Nietzsche failed at precisely the point where he succeeded, for he predicated his superman on Godlessness. To put it simply: no God, no Superman. One cannot become a superman by inflating one's ego. For it is God who confers on a human being the qualities that cause him to be regarded as superior. It is the love of God that attracts us towards Him, and the more we love Him, the more we submit to His commandments. By being meek, humble, and obedient to God, we make ourselves a window unto God's light. If you're familiar with the computer term "user-transparent," we have to make ourselves transparent to God. Only then will we be invested with the qualities that will cause others to regard us as a superior human being. The slightest arrogance, and God will strip from us the qualities He had invested us with. For they are not ours, but on loan from God. The highest point of achievement, the Station of Praise which belongs only to the Prophet, is achieving perfection in being a humble servant of God—easier said than done.

Of course, there can be different degrees of God-realization. And at any given time there will be someone who is the most realized of all. The lesser ones are then able to recognize him as perfect. One Sufi master, for example, said: "The fountain of spirituality gushes out from Effendi. We all fill our jugs from that source, and distribute it to the people." Said another, now deceased: "He is our [President]. Our electricity comes from him, from that great power station in Ankara."

Paranormal Events

Ouspensky called his book on Gurdjieff *In Search of the Miraculous*. What does "miraculous" mean?

When an event is sufficiently out of the ordinary that it stands in a class by itself, we call that event "miraculous." What, then, are we going to call that situation where miraculous events keep going on day after day, month after month, year after year? In other words, what are we to call that condition where the nonordinary becomes ordinary?

Skeptics will call it impossible. Others will call it highly doubtful. I call it the perfect flowering of Mohammedan sainthood.

Interview any one of the Master's followers, and you will hear one or more such accounts. I, too, could relate any number of interesting tales. Just as an example, let me relate what a friend of the Master told me:

Years ago, he was a tenant in a house owned by Mother Hajar. The Kayhans themselves lived a distance away, say 50 or 60 meters. One evening, as he was performing his Prayer, he heard a few knocks on the door and Grandpa Kayhan calling out his name. However, he could not interrupt his Prayer, so when he was finished he went over to the Kayhans' house. Mother Hajar and Effendi were sitting. "I'm sorry I couldn't open the door to you," he said to the Master. Mother Hajar gave him a queer look. "What are you talking about?" she asked. "I was doing my Prayer and I heard Effendi knock on the door and call out my name," he answered. "You're a strange man," Mother Hajar told him. "Effendi hasn't left this room. He suggested to me that we should go over and visit you, and I told him it was late. 'Fine,' he said, 'then we'll call him and he'll come over.' And now here you are. He hasn't moved from his spot all this while." Effendi's only comment was to smile, and invite his friend to sit down.

This, however, is not the point. What mattered was the Master himself, and not whatever secondary manifestations happened to be occurring around his vortex. People too often become fixated on such matters, not knowing that these are actually voices of the Sirens, hindrances to spiritual progress. The focus should be not on the miraculous, but on the ethical.

Of necessity, this approach also precludes the possibility of conducting scientific research "on" the Master. Suggest the idea to the least of his visitors, and they would have thought you were out of your mind. Even the idea of hooking up EEGs and predicting cards smacks of sacrilege and is tantamount to reducing their subject to the status of a mere psychic. Doctors inspecting the Master's anatomy years ago came to the conclusion that he should be clinically dead. What further miracle could one need?

His Death

For years and years, I was obsessed by one thought, and one thought only: death, and hence departure, being inevitable, I must do whatever I can to ensure that the Master survives as long as possible.

To this end I devoted whatever means were at my disposal. His devotees, humanity, the entire universe were all in need of this Man, I thought. At all costs, this unique phenomenon must be preserved, and if his life-span could not be extended indefinitely, then it must at least be stretched to the maximum possible. The Master was very old and sick. He needed his rest, and the constant stream of people coming to his door taxed his energies and his health. He never had a restful night, and yet, come daylight, he would be at least partially rested.

The stream of visitors would start early in the morning. He would accept them all, forbid us from preventing their entry, and heed and try to help the slightest trouble of even an ant. He would resolve the most intractable problems with the greatest of ease. The grind would continue late into the evening. When the last visitor had departed, I would watch him prostrate on his bed, his frail frame utterly exhausted, lying as if dead. It was obvious that this routine could not go on forever. Yet we all refused to contemplate—to even consider—the inevitable.

As a result of this situation, I found myself on the horns of an excruciating dilemma. On one hand I deemed the Master so important that I would have televised him and his teachings to the entire world, if I could. Yet on the other hand, he was so tired and ill that I did not want him to waste one breath, one word, to a single person. To this day, I have not found a solution, a way out. By now it is too late anyway.

The Master had been in ill health for many years. Looking back now, we can see that in the final months he was tidying up his affairs, telling far-off visitors that they would not be seeing him again, putting the finishing touches on his life's work. Of these he breathed not a word to those close to him and in his attendance.

His death was preceded by a week's illness. He was taken to the hospital emergency ward on August 3, and passed away around 10 P.M. that same evening. We had all been hopeful that he would survive, for several months more at the very least, and at first I refused to believe he had died. When I was convinced, I knew that death had finally won, and I had lost.

The Funeral Prayer was performed with a minimum number of people the next morning (Tuesday) at 10:30 A.M., and the Master was laid to rest in his final resting place. As we carried his coffin, it was raised so high that I had to stand on my toes, and even then my fingertips could only barely touch it. This in itself is remarkable, for I am not at all short by Turkish standards.

The Lessons for Us All

Perhaps the first, the most significant, lesson for us from the Master's example is a message of hope. If he, a human being, could achieve this, any human being can do it. Perhaps not to the fullest extent. But to the limits that our individual constitution will allow. Every human being is born as an incredible gift, as a stupendous potential. So pacified have we become by the doldrums of everyday mundane life that we do not even stop to consider what business we have here on Earth. Why weren't we created as birds? Or butterflies? If we were created as human beings, what role does a human being play in the vast design of the universe? What, for heaven's sake, are we here *for?*

If we can shake off the hibernation that has us in its grip, we will realize that a more magnificent destiny can be ours than are dreamt of in our philosophies. Perhaps not everyone can achieve it to an equal degree, just as not everyone can win an Olympic medal. But everyone can do something better than where they're at. If we've spent our lives in suspended animation to this day, at least from now on let us try to wake up.

The next lesson of Effendi is ethics, and herein lies the crux. He was the most ethical person of the highest morality I have ever known. And *that*, he disclosed to me, was the difference that made the difference. Morality was what set him apart from other gurus. This was the foundation on which all else rested; meditation techniques, psychospiritual exercises, specialized knowledge all came later, and were useless without morality.

This, of course, brings in the Sufi notion of "courtesy" (*adab*), which is a refinement of salutary conduct. A friend who has traveled far and wide and met masters of various religions told me after the Master's death that no matter which Islamic Sufi master he visited, they all wore this same garment of courtesy. With other religions there was no standard—each guru was unique and different from the others. And Effendi possessed that courtesy to the highest degree.

Further, the Master pinpointed what causes the ultimate ruin of one's ethics: illicit gain and illicit sex. *Illicit gain and illicit sex*—Effendi never tired of repeating that it was these two we had to be the most wary of, and that the final ruin of humanity, thermonuclear Armageddon, would be the end result of these two.

Illicit pecuniary gain is self-explanatory. Sexual relationships should occur only between lawfully married men and women. Even an atheist can benefit from this advice, provided he heeds it.

A person in control of his hand and his lust and who in addition performs the Formal Prayer (*salat* or *namaz*) has, according to the Master, all the makings of a Sufi saint (a friend of God). From that point onwards, it would be the individual efforts of the seeker, plus the grace of God, which would dictate the outcome.

In order to travel this course, three things are needed: a job, a spouse, and faith. Notice that these correspond to the three requirements above: a job provides honest income, a spouse means a home, a family, and a healthy sexual relationship, and one wouldn't perform the daily Formal Prayers without faith.

◗━◗

The Master is no longer with us, but I shall always cherish his fond memory. If not for him, I should never have realized that the existential problem posed by Nietzsche had been resolved by the Sufis. In a world too often ruled by lovelessness, his universal love and compassion taught me what it means to be human in the best sense of the word.

I have only one more thing to say. *Love one another*, love even an ant.

Introduction

The lips of Pharaoh say:"I am the Truth." It is a lie.
The lips of Hallaj say:"I am the Truth," and it is light.
—Rumi

The title of this book has a built-in double meaning, and this epigraph by Rumi sums it up. Two persons can say exactly the same thing, yet one may be speaking the truth, the other a falsehood. In one sense, "The Station of No Station" refers to a station that is nonexistent, and hence nowhere at all—a dead end, a *cul-de-sac*. In another sense, it refers to a station that transcends all stations, and hence is the greatest station of all. The reference to Pharaoh concerns his claim to deity in his contest with Moses, for he told his people: "I am your greatest Lord" (79:24). The second reference is to the great Sufi, Mansur al-Hallaj, who said: "I am the Truth." Hallaj was executed for this slip of the tongue, of course, yet other famous Sufis have uttered quite similar things while escaping unscathed. There is a background to Hallaj's utterance, but what really concerns us here is the difference between the claim of an ordinary man, however great or powerful, and that of a truly realized human being. Pharaoh finally came to a bad end, and the only reason Hallaj was punished was that he made a claim similar to Pharaoh's, which was liable to be misunderstood. The two could easily be confused. It takes a mystic of Rumi's stature to discern the difference.

Rumi's contrast of Pharaoh versus Hallaj bears a certain resemblance to the contrast between Nietzsche and Rumi, or any Sufi saint in general.

The Role of Nietzsche

In certain respects, which I propose to elucidate in this book, Nietzsche is the key mind of the nineteenth century. He is the gateway to our entire modern and postmodern era. Every so often throughout history, an individual emerges who seemingly embodies all the accomplishments and problems of his age. Nietzsche was one such individual: he served as a node. Whether consciously or unconsciously, he gave expression to all the successes and failures that have occurred since then. This is no mean achievement, and my initial suspicion that he would be worth studying was well rewarded, as I hope you will concur.

But why Nietzsche? Why not anyone else?

It is not my intention to summarize his biography. He has been called the first modern, and we would not be far wrong in calling him the first postmodern man as well. The complexity of his personality reflected the strength and problems of the individual soul in passage. And his thought has permeated our culture to such a degree, or he was so possessed by the spirit of the times, the *zeitgeist,* that today we are all Nietzscheans to one extent or other. A recent movement, for example—the extropians—could justifiably be termed neo-Nietzschean. Nietzsche's influence, or his embodiment of our predicament, has been far from marginal. It is possible to discern Nietzschean elements even in the virtual world of cyberspace.

One thing we should carefully note is that Nietzsche was not only a great philosopher; he was also a great psychologist, perhaps the first in the modern sense, with himself as his primary subject. No less an authority than C.G. Jung has acknowledged Nietzsche's influence on himself, Freud, and Adler. We would be committing a serious error were we to imagine that his writings—and especially *Thus Spoke Zarathustra*—pertained to philosophy alone. He inhabited that narrow, sparsely populated isthmus where psychology and philosophy meet. Followers of his philosophy have a hard time coping with this other facet of his work.

Nietzsche's father—a parson—died when he was an infant, and he grew up in the stifling religious atmosphere of his grandmother and sisters. He reacted to the rigid discipline and spent the rest of his life trying to heal the wounds. He found the anti-world, anti-sex orientation of established religion suffocating. But it was in prefiguring modernity and its aftermath that his main importance would be felt.

The Universe of Signs

Traditionally, the universe and everything in it were considered to be "signs"—pointers to something beyond. To borrow a term from Kant, behind every phenomenon there was the *noumenon*—its essence, its reality.

In evolving a technological civilization, man distanced himself from nature and thus from the signs. The world was already a veil, and man constructed a second veil.

But this was not enough, for, as postmodern thought (most notably in the person of Jean Beaudrillard) has recognized, we have created artificial worlds within the artificial cocoon that technology provides—*simulacra*. Disneyworld is one such construct, an artificial microcosm containing everything from the tropics to Main Street, U.S.A. But it goes further. Not content with visiting ancient cities in Disneyworld, we have transported entire environments into cyberspace.

Thus, as if the veil of nature were not confusing enough, man has added veil upon artificial veil until, at the present remove, he has lost all sight of a way out of the Labyrinth. In fact, he is unable even to perceive of it as a labyrinth.

The distinctive characteristic of postmodern culture is that *it accepts at face value this apparent lack of depth, thus dissolving the distance between signs and meaning.* That distance has collapsed; the pointers point to nothing but themselves. They have become self-referential. (And—a note for the mathematically inclined—where there is self-reference, paradox lurks not far behind.) We conceive of the universe as a gigantic Hollywood prop—behind which there is nothing.

It is more difficult to convince ourselves that the same thing holds within us: that there is nothing beyond the "I," for we at least have dreams, portals to other realities. Here, we have succeeded by conditioning ourselves into fancying that "I" (the mind, the Freudian subconscious, etc.) is, as it were, a secretion of the physical brain or identical with it, beyond which there is again nothing.

To cut a long story short, modernity "is caught up in an increasingly complete eradication of meaning,"[9] and when modernity, too, loses its meaning, *it abolishes itself*—there is no sense left in modernity, or anything else.

This recognition, however, has to be qualified in two different ways. The first is that meaning cannot be *utterly* eradicated, for the simple reason that it is coded into the fabric of the universe. Lesser, residual meanings continue to exist even after Meaning (with a capital M) has been argued out of existence. Additionally, man is the only being gifted with the sense of meaning. The psychologist Victor Frankl pointed out that man could not live without meaning, and that his very mental stability was predicated on his ability to discover it.

The second qualification is that the lifting of restrictions and rules, both heralded and welcomed by Nietzsche, has both a liberating and a disorienting effect. The denial of depth in the external world is reflected in a denial of depth to our inner world. This is interesting from the mystical point of view because people's sense of selfhood is shaken, forcing a confrontation with our selves, and a re-evaluation becomes possible. Sufism has already charted the map for such a rethinking, should we choose to follow that road. For the *deconstruction of the self,* in a positive sense, is one of the main agendas of Sufism. Thus, in our present predicament, we may also find the hope of making a fresh start.

For Nietzsche, however, the eradication of meaning led to nihilism. And this was both liberation and a horror. His whole life was shaped by the overwhelming formula: "God is dead." Once you accept this, all you will be left with is an empty shell of a universe—which is none other than nihilism, as Nietzsche clearly understood.

He tried to heal the damage of this toxic assertion, to go beyond it, by positing a goal for man: the Superman. This is Nietzsche's crucial contribution, and we shall have much to say about it later on. In this, he was able to point to a target that the greatest minds before him had been working towards. Not surprisingly, we first hear of Nietzsche's Superman (*übermensch*) early in Goethe's *Faust,* Part I (published in 1808), which is how the Earth Spirit addresses Faust. As *Faust II* has shown, it is Faustian man who ushers in modernity.

The essence of the modernist project is the *reinvention of man*[10]: "Man makes himself." All the religions and philosophies of old have been superseded, and the image of man fostered by them has been swept away. Man should begin reconstructing himself and building a new morality, based on the use of his reason alone. Granted, there is something heroic in this. Nietzsche has his Zarathustra cry, "Break, my brethren, break these *new* tablets, too!" (It sounds like the battle hymn of Mao's perpetual revolution.) He is against any rules that bind man and limit his freedom.

Yet there is a hidden trapdoor in the "death of God" assertion. It looks like a purely philosophical statement, but it has unexpected repercussions on human psychology. And, because of a collectivity of psyches, its effects are also carried over into sociology. From the Sufic viewpoint, this assertion and the goal of the superhuman are at cross-purposes to, and hence counteract, each other. The result is a static tension that really does not lead us anywhere except a "double-bind," to use Gregory Bateson's coinage. Or perhaps it would be better to say that the assumption defeats the goal.

A person cannot achieve the superhuman condition alone, any more than he can pull himself up by his own bootstraps. If you're in a pit and can't climb out, you need help from outside.

Lacking knowledge about a critical factor of the human self, which the Sufis have elaborated on, the struggle to become a Superman results only in a super-inflated ego. The outcome is complete absorption in one's ego, a monster rather than a Superman. And it is to this situation that the first sense of the book's title applies: the goal is negated, vitiated, and one ends up—nowhere.

Man and God

There is one insight of Nietzsche's that the Sufis, and even all mystics, would wholeheartedly accept: that *man is a bridge between the subhuman and superhuman.* They would, however, perhaps choose to alter the phrasing to read as follows: *man is a bridge extended between animal and God.* For man in his present condition is unfinished. He is but a seed, with the potential to grow into a tree.

It turns out, then, that this and the preceding considerations make Nietzsche a good candidate for Sufic analysis! At times, it seems as if Nietzsche were trying to rediscover Sufism. The insights gained from the timeless science of Sufism can help us understand exactly where Nietzsche succeeded and where he stumbled.

But this is not simply about him alone. Nietzsche's struggle is also our own. And as a person living in this age, it was mine as well, until I encountered a branch of Sufism that I have not met with in any book, nor indeed anywhere else. By using its teachings to investigate Nietzsche's successes and problems more closely, we shall be able to address our relationship with the transcendent and immanent divinity.

We have all read about Superman in the comics, to be sure, or seen superheroes in movies. But it was only after I met the Sufi masters of Central Anatolia that I was able to invest Nietzsche's term with meaning—to see what it really meant. The sense was both his and yet not his.

The insight I arrived at was that the Superman had to be *man possessed of supraconsciousness*. Imagine my surprise when I discovered that this could only be achieved via a super morality!

Man has the choice, the possibility, the freedom to develop— or to sell himself short. Nietzsche symbolizes the unrealized potential of a soul striving to transcend animal limitations.

Furthermore, Sufism is possible now, today, at this very moment, and will remain so. Even though we have trodden Nietzsche's trail, we shall be fulfilling and not violating his deepest aspirations by going beyond it. That is, man can save himself but must strive to do so—God won't do it overtly.

Secular Science

A strong dose of science has gone into my constitution, probably more than most people have. And I would be the last to deny the multifold boons of science and technology. At the same time, however, an infatuation with secular science should not blind us to the appreciation that a hammer is not quite the right tool for mending a watch. When the phenomenal successes of science dazzled all and sundry, it was called upon to answer the question "Where did all this come from?"—with the further constraint that the answer had to contain no reference to God. There was no choice but to attribute existence and life—and hence, consciousness as well—to chance. It went unnoticed that chance, by this attribution, was being elevated to omnipotence, and that science was being used to do bad metaphysics, something it was never intended for. The important point here is that chance has become the dominant paradigm of *all* our thinking today.

Overview

The plan of this book is as follows: Chapter 1 introduces our main theme, Nietzsche's singular insight, and goes on to discuss God, the Base Self (a concept of the first importance in Sufism), and the Superman. A sideways glance at Darwin highlights the extent to which chance has become a blanket answer for all too many things in our culture. The chapter ends by drawing out some of the implications—social and historical—of atheism.

Nietzsche was a profound thinker. Doing justice to him calls for sophisticated analysis. As a consequence, this is the most involved chapter of the book, and heavy going in places. These parts can be skipped if desired, but my hope is that the persevering reader will not go unrewarded.

The Sufi view of man and universe yields surprising insights that are dealt with in Chapter 2, which outlines the grand design of the universe and man's place in it. This leads into the relationship between ethics and enlightenment from the standpoint of Sufism. (To put it in a nutshell: no ethics, no enlightenment.)

By this time, the treatment has progressed to Chapter 3, where we can introduce Sufi psychology (in the sense of "self-knowledge"). The Base Self is examined in greater detail for the light it sheds on such diverse subjects as psychology, sociology, and modernity. This level of selfhood, however, is the base for more advanced stages of the self, leading to the higher reaches of human evolution. These higher stages are outlined briefly in Chapter 4.

There are two main branches in the Sufi path, the way of the self and the way of the spirit. These are dealt with in Chapters 4 and 5, respectively. The latter treats the subtle body and its psychic anatomy. The way of the spirit, however, must ultimately rest on self-improvement, so that the way of the self has higher priority. Chapter 6 outlines the practical, do-it-yourself methods of Sufism, methods that are inherently safe. The chapter starts with the three principles a Sufi—whether student or saint—must fulfill, as outlined in the teachings of the Master. Various methods have been used throughout history by those wishing to attain enlightenment, and we focus on two of these, Formal Prayer and Fasting.

In Chapter 2, we see why spiritual transformation is not feasible in a void of ethics. The Great Work of enlightenment, therefore, has both a psychological and a social aspect. Chapter 7 explores this social dimension. Salman Rushdie's controversial novel, *The Satanic Verses,* serves as a springboard for a discussion of Islamic politics and the relationship between ethics and democracy from a Sufic standpoint—democracy being associated with a specific human type, the democratic personality. It is seldom realized that this personality type is a major goal of religion. The chapter ends with a Sufic (not to say Islamic) proposal as to how poverty may be eradicated on a global scale, and how this can fortify democracy (or, in more general terms, the "open society").

Having traveled this far, we can now go into the "meat" of

Sufism, i.e., the higher reaches of human consciousness. Chapter 8 concludes the book by dealing with the mystical concept of spiritual embryogenesis (from the viewpoint of Sufism and other traditions), and by speaking about the Unspeakable—to the extent that this is possible. But as Wittgenstein observed, "Whereof one may not speak, thereof one must remain silent." And that is where the book signs off.

As it stands, the book constitutes a portal to Sufism. It uses an approach that has—to my knowledge—never been attempted before, enabling a better appreciation of this tantalizing subject.

Science has become so influential in the past few centuries that dominant scientific paradigms do not fail to have an effect on the social mindset sooner or later. Modernity was influenced by nineteenth-century positivism, which held that there is only a single truth, and it is what you can measure by your five senses plus a yardstick.

The beginning of the twentieth century saw the advent of two great scientific theories that were to dominate the remainder: relativity and quantum mechanics. Naturally, it takes some time for abstract scientific concepts to percolate down to general social consciousness, and the effect is so indirect that many remain unaware of the connection. Roughly half a century after Heisenberg stated his famous uncertainty principle, and a quarter-century after Hugh Everett III's many-worlds interpretation of quantum mechanics, postmodernism emerged as a reaction to modernity, to the tyranny of reason and "single vision." It was marked by moral and cultural relativism, the coexistence of contending viewpoints about reality, and the realization that uncertainty lies at the very root of things, leading to equal opportunity for all viewpoints. Gödel's proof that all mathematical systems must remain incomplete in some essential sense provided further grist for this mill.

To my mind, this does not rule out an Absolute. Rather, it suggests that there can be only one Absolute. Einstein did not show that everything is relative; he showed that there are things which remain invariant under varying conditions—the agenda, indeed, of all science. But the only true Absolute must be transcendent, beyond all finitude and relativity, beyond the physical universe that is draped like a tapestry over our senses.

Where does all this leave us? Our "postmodern world" is both in debt to Nietzsche and very different from the world he saw. There is something a lot more "playful" in our situation, whereas he had to experience and suffer the full force of modernity. He lived in a "twilight of the idols" that had begun crashing down, and he had to struggle against titanic forces at the brink of an abyss. On the other hand, we live in an even dimmer twilight zone, a pleasant limbo where the abyss has somehow been patched over. All the cracks that Nietzsche saw with electrifying clarity have seemingly disappeared. Together with the end of the cold war, this has led to the euphoria of the last decade of the twentieth century, leaving many with the impression that the "end of history" is at hand.

But the fact that a thing is obscured does not make it any less real. Rather, it makes it more dangerous, because forewarned is forearmed, and in our end-of-the-century elation, we threw precaution to the winds. And now a new millennium has dawned, in which we have to take stock of the situation and chart new trails.

The abyss that spelled Nietzsche's undoing may yet get the better of us, too. In order to understand how and why, let us begin by considering the issues he faced.

❥❥❥

This introduction has provided an overview to the book, establishing the importance of Nietzsche in the history of ideas, agreeing with his emphasis on the need for a "reinvention of man," but raising the question of the true "signification" of the universe. This question arises not just in the context of a secular science but a science that realizes a higher potential implicit in man—one that helps man cross a bridge contained within himself. Chapter 1 now looks at Nietzsche's predicament in more detail.

1

NIETZSCHE, GOD, AND DOOMSDAY: THE CONSEQUENCES OF ATHEISM[11]

*Reason divorced of knowledge of the
divine burns into itself, like acid.*
—Seyyed Hossein Nasr[12]

*Do you know what fear and loneliness mean? . . .You will see
nothing in that expanse of eternal emptiness, you will not hear
your own step, you will find nothing solid for you to rest upon.*
—Mephistopheles[13]

In the Mouth of Madness

Nietzsche saw it coming. "The story I have to tell," he wrote, "is the history of the next two centuries. . . . For a long time now our whole civilization has been driving, with a tortured intensity growing from decade to decade, as if towards a catastrophe: restlessly, violently, tempestuously, like a mighty river desiring the end of its journey, without pausing to reflect, indeed fearful of reflection. . . . Where we live, soon nobody will be able to exist."[14]

Nietzsche's was a mind that thought so deeply and with such intensity that it threw off sparks and crackled like a high-voltage generator. Poised on the brink of the twentieth century, in which so many grand ideals were shattered, he saw it all in the crystal ball of his mind, and the abyss he beheld was so horrifying that he desperately tugged at the emergency brakes, vainly trying to stop the runaway train. "There will be wars," he prophesied, "such as have never been waged on earth." And again: "I foresee something terrible, Chaos everywhere. Nothing left which is of any value; nothing which commands: Thou shalt!"[15]

Nietzsche was no stranger to paradox and contradiction. He was simultaneously the opponent, proponent, and victim of the nihilism he foresaw. His was a mind at war against his soul, a spirit locked in titanic struggle with the intellect. A student of Sufi psychology might observe that his ego—his "Me," his egotistical self—gained control over his mind, and the latter thwarted all attempts of his spirit to elevate itself by placing before it a self-defeating intellectual obstacle around which it could find no way.

One observation, one singular realization was the motivating force behind all his struggles, driving him on feverishly until his mind burned itself out trying to devise an escape. This was a formula, simply stated in three monosyllabic words, yet earth-shaking in its implications: "God is dead."[16]

Nowadays, of course, lots of people believe in this notion without giving it a second thought. Yet the genius of Nietzsche was able to foresee all it implied, to draw most, if not indeed all, of the conclusions that would follow from the notion's acceptance. It is for this reason that we must inspect it more closely, and in order to do this we must begin with what Nietzsche actually said.

The formula "God is dead" appears, to be sure, in *Thus Spoke Zarathustra,* but it makes its first appearance in Section 108 of *The Joyous Science* (1882),[17] written two years before

Zarathustra during Nietzsche's so-called positivist period. Not only is God dead, he says, but we must banish even his shadow from the caves of our minds. There follow aphorisms extolling science and a "naturalistic" world-view. And then, suddenly, the concept appears full-blown in Section 125, under the title of "the Madman." The madman is actually Nietzsche himself, who casts the former in the image of a new Diogenes. The following extract contains the gist of it.

> Have you not heard of that madman who lit a lantern in the bright morning hours, ran to the market place, and cried incessantly: "I seek God! I seek God!" . . .
> The madman jumped into their midst and pierced them with his eyes. "Whither is God?" he cried; "I will tell you. *We have killed him*—you and I. All of us are his murderers. But how did we do this? How could we drink up the sea? Who gave us the sponge to wipe away the entire horizon? What were we doing when we unchained the earth from its sun? Whither is it moving now? Whither are we moving? Away from all suns?"

The madman asks questions which imply that we are continually plunging, backward, sideward, forward, in all directions. There is no longer any up or down. We are straying as through an infinite nothing. We feel the breath of empty space; it has become colder. The night is continually closing in on us—we need to light lanterns in the morning. Then he continues:

> "God is dead. God remains dead. And we have killed him.
> "How shall we comfort ourselves, the murderers of all murderers? What was holiest and mightiest of all that the world has yet owned has bled to death under our knives: who will wipe this blood off us? What water is there for us

to clean ourselves? . . . Is not the greatness of this deed too great for us? Must we ourselves not become gods simply to appear worthy of it?"

Here the madman fell silent and looked again at his listeners. . . . "I have come too early," he said then; "my time is not yet. This tremendous event is still on its way, still wandering; it has not yet reached the ears of men. Lightning and thunder require time; the light of the stars requires time; deeds, though done, still require time to be seen and heard. This deed is still more distant from them than the most distant stars—*and yet they have done it themselves.*"[18]

But what does Nietzsche mean when he says "God is dead"? What kind of psychology does it indicate? In 1887, in the second edition of *The Joyous Science,* Nietzsche added Book Five to the original, which begins with Section 343 and the phrase: "The greatest recent event—that God is dead, that the belief in the Christian God has become unbelievable. . . . " As translator and eminent Nietzsche scholar Walter Kaufmann points out: "This clause is clearly offered as an explanation of 'God is dead.'"[19] In *The Antichrist* (1888), Nietzsche is more specific: "The Christian conception of God . . . is one of the most corrupt conceptions of God arrived at on earth. . . . "[20] And, when he was already close to insanity, he called himself "the Anti-Christ."[21]

We may now pause here and think. Nietzsche obviously means that the *Christian notion* of God is dead, that this notion has become unbelievable. But to extrapolate from this to the assertion that God Almighty, the Lord of the universe and of all the worlds, now cannot be believed in, is as incorrect as it is dangerous.

What typifies the Christian notion of God? Basically it postulates a set of beliefs and makes certain attributions regarding the relationship between God and Jesus. These concepts, according to Nietzsche, set the Christian idea of God apart from other forms of monotheism and make it increasingly untenable to support.[22]

Nietzsche argued that morality without religion is impossible: "All purely moral demands without their religious basis must needs end in nihilism."[23] Moral systems created by man without reference to God are actually unconscious regressions to religious morality. This is true even of atheists who are highly moral: an operating system that has been the engine of a civilization for two thousand years still powers their neurons. With the demise of faith, furthermore, not only morality but the universe of meanings begins to collapse, and since man cannot live without meaning, he tries to resurrect meaning under different headings. Richard Wilhelm once equated the Chinese concept of Tao with the German word *Sinn,* or meaning,[24] and in the same way we may say that God is the meaning, the *esprit* (both the spirit and the meaning) of the universe. In order to believe in God and practice moral behavior, we cannot wait for the resolution of fine theological points.

Yet we must also recognize that Nietzsche's rejection of God goes deeper—starting from "a critique of the *Christian conception of God,*"[25] he generalizes to all forms of monotheism, accusing all religions of pious fraud, of "the holy lie."[26] His hatred of Christianity is so profound that it overflows beyond its proper bounds to encompass other religions as well. It then becomes necessary to draw out the implications of this stance. Let us start with his attitude towards science.

Nietzsche and Science

Nietzsche's relationship with science was ambivalent. While he recognized its utility and praised its naturalism, he also regarded science as being based on faith.

To make it possible for this discipline to begin must
there not be some prior conviction . . . ? We see that science also rests on faith; there simply is no science "without
presuppositions."[27]

And in this, Nietzsche is right. Michael Polanyi, himself a scientist and a profound thinker on the philosophy of science,
found belief to be an essential requirement of science: "no one
can become a scientist unless he presumes that the scientific doctrine and method are fundamentally sound and that their ultimate premises can be unquestioningly accepted."[28] "Any
account of science which does not explicitly describe it as something we believe in is essentially incomplete and a false pre-
tense."[29] Nietzsche continues:

> . . . from where [does] science [take] its unconditional
> faith or conviction on which it rests, that truth is more
> important than any other thing, including every other con-
> viction? . . . "I will not deceive, not even myself"; *and with
> that we stand on moral ground.* [30]

Thus Nietzsche proves himself to be a *moralist of knowledge.*
There is no "objective," i.e., morally neutral knowledge. If we
were to adopt a Sufic standpoint, we would see that Nietzsche
demonstrates this from two perspectives. The perspective given
above, that knowledge is sublime truth, is the standpoint of the
Purified Self. Elsewhere, Nietzsche also demonstrates "that
knowledge . . . is the subtlest guise of the Will to Power [of the
egotistical self, as it is called in Sufi terminology]; and that *as a
manifestation of the will it is liable to be judged morally.*"[31]

Thus the question "Why science?" leads back to the
moral problem: *Why have morality at all* when life, nature,

46

and history are "not moral"? No doubt, those who are truthful in that audacious and ultimate sense that is presupposed by faith and science *thus affirm another world* than the world of life, nature, and history; and insofar as they affirm this "other world"—look, must they not by the same token negate its counterpart, this world, *our* world?[32]

As Edwin A. Burtt has shown, the world of science is abstracted from this world, a "Platonic" world based on mathematics.[33]

—But you will have gathered what I am driving at, namely, that it is still a *metaphysical faith* upon which our faith in science rests—that even we seekers after knowledge today, we godless anti-metaphysicians still take our fire, too, from . . . that Christian faith which was also the faith of Plato, that God is the truth, that truth is divine.[34]

Following his own logic, Nietzsche necessarily comes to the point where God must be eradicated from his belief system, which is the antithesis of faith:

—But what if this should become more and more incredible . . . if God himself should prove to be our most enduring lie?[35]

This forms the bedrock for Nietzsche's earlier comments:

The total character of the world, however, is in all eternity chaos—in the sense not of a lack of necessity but of a lack of order, arrangement, form, beauty, wisdom, and whatever other names there are for our aesthetic anthropomorphisms. . . . Let us beware of saying that there are laws in nature. There are only necessities: there is nobody who commands, nobody who obeys, nobody who trespasses. Once you know that there are no purposes, you also know that there is no accident; for it is only beside a world of purposes that the word "accident" has any meaning.[36]

Thus, the denial of God has driven Nietzsche to deny science, the laws of nature, the existence of order and even of causality. There is no purpose in the world, only "chaos." Instead of "law," Nietzsche substitutes "necessity." But what is this but another name for "law"?

It is interesting to note that Nietzsche is not alone in the conclusions he reaches. Before him, David Hume trod the same path, and in his efforts to deny God did away even with the connection between cause and effect. Thus, as Professor Jacques Barzun notes, Hume arrived at a distrust of science and religion alike: "Hume's last word of doubt on religion carries with it such a doubt about the mind of man that the certainty of science goes down in shipwreck too."[37] It was Kant who, transcending Hume, slipped a fresh foundation under the work of science.

Strikingly, we find the same attitude in Nietzsche. In *The Will to Power,* he states: "the psychological necessity for a belief in causality lies in the inconceivability of an event divorced from intent. . . . The belief in [causes] falls with the belief in [purpose]."[38] Thus the denial of God leads to the denial of causality, the basic underpinning of science. The world is not an organism, it is not even a machine. Even grammar does not escape his attacks, for it is a system of rules and order, and the repository of a hidden belief in causality.[39]

Why? Why do both Hume and Nietzsche, in their over-zealous efforts to deny God, end up debauching science as well? Because their denial of God is dependent on the denial of any order whatsoever in the universe. Because they knew that science took its origin, and is still based on, a world in which order pre-vails. If the world is chaos, there can be no order, and hence no laws either of nature or of science. (In our day, however, even the word "chaos" is being redefined, as mathematicians and scien-tists discern hidden order in chaos.) For the existence of any kind of laws presupposes a Lawgiver, and indeed the originators of modern science—Newton, Descartes, Leibnitz, etc.—quite open-ly expressed their faith in a Divine Lawmaker. In order to deny the latter, Hume, Nietzsche, and those who follow their path must deny the existence of *any kind of order at all*. But without such order, the whole enterprise of science falls down, for it is then senseless to seek laws, order, or pattern in a disordered world. Nietzsche borders on Orwellian Newspeak in his implied conclusion—"truth is a lie"—and falls into the same rut that he so despises in those who confuse mortality and immortality (see "Misconceptions About God" below). Yet paradoxically, Nietzsche was also genius enough to recognize that his nihilistic teaching (and Zarathustra's) is a "rebound from 'God is truth' to the fanatical faith 'All is false'."[40]

But is all this true? "The proof of the pudding is in the eat-ing." Science *works*—it is the most successful enterprise in the history of humanity. Even chance, even probability, has its laws and is not chaos. In that case, it makes sense to view the world as an ordered place where laws—laws of science, laws of nature—hold. So it makes sense, in turn, to talk about a Lawgiver—which Newton, Copernicus, *et al.* told us right from the very beginning, and which we would never have lost sight of had we not extended our debunking of the Christian conception of God to God Himself. The common alternative is to assume that we ourselves project order onto the universe, which is a form of solipsism. In that case, though, the basis for an objective universe and materialism collapses. Even granting the point of solipsism, however, if man finds meaning within himself, where does he dredge up this meaning from? For according to Sufism, God is both Within us and Without, so that we approach God even when we go within. God is both transcendent and immanent. Contrary to what Nietzsche thought, He is not just incarnate in Jesus, and not just beyond the universe.

Having denied the existence of all order, all laws, Nietzsche then turns around and postulates his own "law" of eternal recurrence—the universe as a finite-state system in infinite time,[41] an endless loop of tape replayed forever—for which there is not the slightest shred of physical evidence. Thus he replaces (as many people after him have also done) all the physics and metaphysics he has overthrown with his own brand of "naturalistic" metaphysics. Assuming that the universe is purely physical, this is the way Nietzsche reintroduces "rebirth" and "immortality"—primal yearnings of the human soul. In Germanic mythology, the world begins anew after the great destruction. The Greek concept of *apokatastasis* or restoration, and the early Christian views on redemption, are similar constructs. As Mircea Eliade has shown in his *Myth of the Eternal Return*, primitives, too, overcome the irreversibility of time by investing it with a cyclic attribute.[42] The cosmic rhythms we observe, such as day and night or the seasons, lead in the end to an extrapolation to the universe as a whole, as evidenced even in the conjecture in modern cosmology of an "oscillating universe." Thus Nietzsche merely rediscovered an age-old concept of man.

One final point. Nietzsche's attempt to proclaim God dead results not only in the denial of truth, of science, but also of life. Had Nietzsche realized this, he would no doubt have deemed it necessary to revise his standpoint, for one of his main objections against Christianity was that it devalued life and this world by emphasizing the existence of—and the happier future state in—a next world. Now observe:

Let us beware of saying that death is opposed to life. The living is merely a type of what is dead, a very rare type.[43]

By reducing spirit to matter and life to death, Nietzsche makes life *an abnormal condition*. Quite inadvertently, he thus devalues and depreciates life in the same manner as those he opposes. And in the practice of lesser minds, such abstract philosophical concepts translate into an effort to kill off living things, to reduce them to their "normal" state. In Thomas Berger's novel *Little Big Man,* an Indian chief says that such men "believe that everything is dead: stones, earth, animals, and people, even their own people. And if, in spite of that, things persist in trying to live, [they] will rub them out."

And hence, as Nietzsche feared, but also advocated in spite of himself, we reach total nihilism—the effort to turn everything into nothing.

Misconceptions About God

Man is mortal, God is immortal. This is a crucial rule by which all forms of monotheism must abide. Man may be spiritually purified and elevated to a "vision of God," but this does not allow us to confuse one with the other.

ON A SUNNY DAY, GO OUT INTO THE SUNSHINE. BATHE IN IT, BE ENLIGHTENED IN IT, BE WARMED BY IT. THEN COME BACK INDOORS AND ASK YOURSELF: "DID I SEE THE SUN?" YES. "DID IT ENLIGHTEN ME?" YES. "DID IT WARM ME UP?" YES.

BUT: "AM I THE SUN?" NO!

The case of God is similar to the case of the sun. No one who has enjoyed a special relationship with God, however close, can claim to be God Himself on the basis of that relationship or experience.

When the Prophet of God died, there was a great commotion.

People could not believe that the event had actually happened. Omar, one of his closest Companions, drew out his sword and threatened to impale anyone who uttered that the Prophet was dead. At this point Abu Bakr, the closest Companion, intervened, and after calming them all down, said: "Those who believe in Mohammed, know that Mohammed is dead. Those who believe in God, know that God is immortal, and cannot die."

Now this is the proper attitude. *And this is the crux of the problem.* For if we equate God with a certain man—granted, a great and wonderful man—then when that man dies, we are justified in saying that "God is dead (or crucified)." Thus when Nietzsche speaks about "the death of God," he is also talking about the death of Christ on the cross.[44] In this sense, Nietzsche's remark is a direct consequence of this dangerous equation and properly belongs not in the nineteenth century, but nineteen centuries ago. Nietzsche displays awareness of this when he says: "We deny God as God. If one were to *prove* this God of the Christians to us, we should be even less able to believe in him. In a formula: *God, as Paul created him, is the negation of God.*"[45]

In this light, consider the unforgettable words of the Master: "God is not man, and man is not God. But God is close to man, and man is close to God." With a deft move of the scalpel, he solved the problem that has been plaguing our civilization for two thousand years: "God has given man many things, He has given him everything, but He has not given him His Godhood." The impossibilities are removed as soon as this is admitted, yet we are not talking about a God who is remote to humankind.

The Mansion and the Houseguests

Two other frequent misconceptions about God concern those on the other side of the fence. The concept of God as a puppet-master or an oriental despot, so often advanced by atheists, is simply wrong. If God had wanted absolute hegemony over man, nothing could have been simpler: He could have created a race of mindless robots. Instead He has given man a mind and free will, and placed him in charge of this planet. But there is no authority without responsibility. Hence man is responsible for what he does on Earth. Free will means that man is free to choose both good and bad: God does not compel man to anything. Man is bound by his circumstances, but he is free to make *moral choices and actions*. If he does something out of compulsion, he is not responsible—which is precisely why Omar, the second Caliph whose penchant for justice was as legendary as that of King Solomon, forgave a destitute man when he stole some food from the marketplace. But free will without guidance is naught, for without guidance man might not be able to tell right from wrong. Hence God has given man *both* free will *and* the right guidance to use that freedom wisely.

But such freedom comes at a price. The price is that man is responsible, and hence accountable, for his actions. For this freedom of will and action means that man can hurt other men, that he can harm other creatures. If man has the license to interfere with God's creation, this does not mean he has the right to destroy or misplace anything.

The following parable is more to the point than the similes of either puppet-master or oriental despot. The rich owner of a country manor has sent various friends of his to stay there during their summer vacation. The trip, however, proves so rough that the guests are afflicted with amnesia by the time they arrive at the mansion. Inside they find rooms full of wondrous objects, tables decked with fruit, and beautiful tapestries. The owner of the house, aware of the difficult passage of his guests, has left a manual on the main table outlining the house rules. One of these rules is that the guests should share in the daily household chores, such as cooking and washing the dishes. Another is that they should show proper love and respect for each other, since they have all been chosen and sent there by the same landlord. It is also good etiquette to remember the landlord from time to time, to contact him and thank him for the beautiful gift he has made to his guests.

So from that point on, it is the guests' collective responsibility to manage the household. But if they fall among each other; if they start quarreling and attacking one another; if they dump their waste in the middle of the living room; if they start swinging from the chandeliers; if they make a hell out of this paradise resort; if they pretend that the landlord does not exist, or pick up the phone and curse him for all their own self-caused troubles; if their response is misery instead of gratitude, then they will have sunk into the depths of discourtesy. And what if the guests ruin the house, if they destroy the furniture? What if *they burn the house down in the end?*

Now this is exactly our situation on Earth. And for this reason if for nothing else, we must question whether all atheistic philosophies provide man with an excuse to shirk his responsibilities and to defile the mansion in which he is a guest—the world—with his abominations.

Nietzsche sees this quite clearly. In *The Twilight of the Idols*, after branding free will an "error," he states: "We deny God; in denying God, we deny accountability. . . . "[46] As Dostoevsky put it: "If there is no God, everything is permitted." *This* is the real reason for denying God: the purpose is not to unveil some profound truth (as it happens, an untruth), but to deliver our egotistical selves from moral qualms and considerations. Eradicate belief in God, and you rip out the root of morality. Nietzsche has deciphered the sequence well: if no God, then no accountability; if no accountability, then no need, indeed no possibility, for morality. It is the next step in this sequence that Nietzsche shrinks away from: without morality, it becomes not merely possible, but inevitable, for us to perpetrate unspeakable monstrosities against each other, against other beings, against nature.[47]

Of course, declaring the death of God has tremendous implications for us, but leaves God Himself untouched. Hence, we will be held to account whether we believe in God or not, and to think we can evade it is simply a delusion. Meanwhile, burying our heads in the ground like an ostrich only serves—by instilling a false sense of relief and license—to increase the dastardly deeds on our account, throwing us ever further "into the red."

One crucial point needs to be borne in mind. In a Holy Tradition of the Prophet, God declares: "I conform [limit] Myself to the opinion that My servant has of Me," which means: "I manifest Myself to a human being (appear to him) only in the form of his belief"—or disbelief. In other words, if a person expects God to act in a certain way, God will generally comply. If a person believes that only blind nature exists, God will act in such a way as to confirm him in his belief. If he believes that the essence of the universe is meaninglessness, God will oblige him. If a person thinks that there is no proof for the existence of God, *God will remove all proof, indeed all possibility of proof,* from his sphere of experience. If man forsakes God, God in turn forsakes man: "As the blind man views God, so God views the blind man."

The Base Self versus God

Let us now follow the consequences of the statement "The belief in God is dead" to its logical conclusions. In this we shall employ a singular insight of Sufi psychology: the existence of the ego, Base Self, or "egotistical self" in man.

What are the basic drives of the egotistical self? They are, first, its material—and by implication its financial—interests, its drive towards sexual satisfaction, and its will to power. All three points were investigated in the nineteenth century by Marx, Freud, and Nietzsche, respectively. The insights of these men cannot be gainsaid. But they all lacked the knowledge that would allow them to integrate the three. And, furthermore, each one reduced questions of cosmic importance to his own discovery regarding a species inhabiting a dust speck in the vast expanses of the universe. Thus, the concept of God was, for Marx, a consequence of what he termed the "superstructure"; for Freud, a "sublimation, projection, or illusion"; and for Nietzsche, a self-deception.

Let us now go back to the egotistical self. Assume that its material needs, food, and comfort are provided for. Assume, too, that its sexual drives have been satisfied. Yet for the Base Self this is not the end but merely a beginning, for it is precisely from this point onward that its further expansion must proceed. Nietzsche's original term for this in *Daybreak* and *The Joyous Science,* the "lust for power" or "love of power" (*machtgelüst*), is more revealing than his later "will to power." And indeed, left to its own devices, the Base Self will try to appropriate more and more power to itself—whether it be political power, social power, or pecuniary power. And Nietzsche, better than Marx or Freud, was able to discern this motivation. (Following in Nietzsche's footsteps, Alfred Adler as well as Bertrand Russell identified power as the motive force in man.) Ahmed Sirhindi (1563-1624), one of the greatest Sufi saints, once explained it this way:

> The self (*nafs*) in its state of impulsiveness (*ammara*) always strives to be superior. . . . It refuses to acknowledge its dependence on and debt to others. This is nothing but a claim to divinity. . . . Indeed, [such a] self will not settle even for partnership with God, but desires to subjugate even Him, to enslave all that exists. It is for this reason

that aiding and abetting this self, the enemy of God, . . . is the greatest of follies and disasters.[48]

Here, the basic motivation of the Base Self stands revealed: *it wants to be God,* even if this is impossible. It desires absolute submission on the part of others.[49]

Now the greatest obstacle in this way is *belief in God Himself.* The selfish ego in man cannot tolerate even God, or perhaps *especially* God, so it will try to abolish belief in God the first chance it gets. In all their merciless unmasking of base motives, Marx, Freud, and Nietzsche never suspected that this was the reason for their atheism, and the subtlest thinkers fell victim to the even subtler tricks of the Base Self. Nietzsche's madman reveals the consequences of "God is dead": " . . . must not we ourselves become gods?" One of Dostoevsky's characters remarks: "If there is no God, then I am God." Nietzsche's following remark, the apogee of hubris, tells it all: "Today I love myself as my god."[50] And indeed, in the final throes of Nietzsche's megalomania, he claimed that he was God.[51]

This Sufic analysis is corroborated by Jungian psychology. In his treatment of Nietzsche's *Zarathustra,* the great psychologist Carl G. Jung remarks:

If you knew what reality that fact possesses which has been called God, you would know that you could not possibly get away from it. But you have lost sight of it; you don't know what that thing means and so it gets at you unconsciously, and then without knowing it you are transformed into God almighty, as happened to Nietzsche. It got into him to such an extent that he went crazy and signed his letters "the dismembered [Dionysos] Zagreus," or "Christ Dionysos," because he became identical with the God he had eliminated. You see, inasmuch as we have eliminated God to a great extent, it is just as if we were all denying the fact that we were hungry, but then we begin to eat each other; we get so hungry that a catastrophe will follow . . . we now think that the progress of thought and the development of the human mind is hampered by the existence of such old prejudices, and we destroy those old forms because we think that we are gods and can do without them. . . . There, of course, is the great danger of any creation: it destroys something, which should not be destroyed, and out of that develop the most catastrophic consequences, as in Nietzsche's case.[52]

Jung goes on to point out Nietzsche's "identification with the deity—the Superman takes the place of the deity."

But there is a further problem to be reckoned with here. Having declared God dead, Nietzsche's self-deification followed as a matter of course. But even this megalomania may not have been his real undoing. For there is yet a final twist, a further step to go: if God is dead, and Nietzsche is God, then Nietzsche is—dead! Dead, and yet alive! (Recall that he refers to himself as "the dismembered," "the crucified.") This short-circuit, this final paradox, must have proved too much of a strain for even the likes of *his* nimble mind, which thereupon committed mental suicide, and he became the ultimate embodiment—or is it the entombment?—of his own reasoning: a dead, shattered mind in a living body.

Thus, it can be seen that in Nietzsche's case, the egotistical self declared its final rebellion by totally blotting out his mind, which it had driven to the point of exhaustion. (This is why Sirhindi says that aiding the Base Self is the greatest folly, the worst disaster.) Like a tool which has outlived its usefulness, it was then broken and thrown away, after all the efforts of his great spirit to achieve salvation had been successfully thwarted by his intellect using the deadly formula: "God is dead." Nietzsche's insanity has been linked with tertiary syphilis, but this—if true—can only have accelerated, not caused, the process.

It is a pity that this had to be the outcome, since Nietzsche had already deduced that "strenuousness," or self-exertion, was the way to go—in Sufi psychology, a cardinal method for cornering the Base Self.

Astoundingly, one side of Nietzsche reached down into the abyss of atheism and nihilism, while with his other side he reached up towards the Sufi ideal of the Perfect Human. It is in this fact that his greatest interest for us lies. Nietzsche's two projects, "God is dead" and the Superman, are mutually incompatible. Through the narrow crack between these two propositions, we are able to catch a glimpse of . . . Sufism.

Which brings us to a discussion of Nietzsche's "Superman."

The Superman

"Man is a rope," says Nietzsche in *Zarathustra*, "suspended between animal and superman—a rope over an abyss."[53] Thus he portrays man as an unfinished, incomplete being. In this he is entirely in accord with Sufi psychology, and with the mystics of all traditions. But just at the point where Nietzsche's ideas begin to show the greatest potential, his project proves self-defeating— for he trips himself up by his continued adherence to "the death of God." Without God, there can be no Superman, no God-realized man, no saint, no man who is close to God. Without that light and guidance, one can only be close to the devil.

In some respects, Nietzsche has intuited the path that leads to a Sufi saint or "friend of God." He talks of "a war against oneself, that is to say, self-control."[54] "The greatest war," said the Prophet of God, "is the war against our selves." In *Human, All Too Human*, Nietzsche recognizes the existence of a "higher self."[55] "The discipline of suffering, of *great* suffering—do you not know that it is *this* discipline alone which has created every elevation of mankind hitherto?"[56] He asks "what type of human being one ought to *breed*"—"This more valuable type has existed often enough already: but as a lucky accident, as an exception, never as *willed*."[57] He talks of a "type of higher species of man, half 'saint', half 'genius'. . . . "[58]

Thus Spoke Zarathustra, in particular, shows how closely Nietzsche was able to approach the truths of Sufi psychology at some points. Couched in dreamlike imagery, it is Nietzsche's spiritual journey and testament. Nietzsche wrote its major parts very quickly in a trancelike state and elaborated upon them afterwards; his subconscious gushed forth onto the paper like water from a broken dam. In Jungian terms, the archetype of the "wise old man" became activated in him in the person of Zarathustra, and in *Ecce Homo* Nietzsche himself speaks of being "merely an incarnation, mouthpiece or medium" for that figure. Yet he appears to have only partially digested or assimilated the insights of the latter; as C.G. Jung notes, lacking the means of modern psychology, Nietzsche does not display awareness in many cases of what the revelations flowing out through his hand really mean.

Zarathustra is replete with symbolism pertaining to the Base Self (called *nafs al-ammara* in Sufism). Not surprisingly, this aspect of *Zarathustra* has gone almost entirely unnoticed, for as Jung observed, "in the west we have no philosophy of the self,"[59] and even a man of his stature was not always able to discern the portent of these symbols (Jung refers to the Base Self as the "shadow" or "inferior man" when he does).

Since Nietzsche is preoccupied with questions of self-surmounting and the Superman, images of the base and higher selves keep surfacing in a highly symbolic form which is quite abstruse, but not indecipherable to Sufic wisdom. The jester (or dwarf) who jumps over the tightrope walker trying to get to the Superman, causing him to fall to his death; "The Ugliest Man" who murders God, because he can't stand the discovery of the ugliness of his innermost depths by all-seeing eyes; the large black snake that bites the young shepherd inside his throat—all these are prime symbols of the Base Self. When the shepherd bites off the head of the snake, i.e., vanquishes his lower self, he laughs as no man has laughed before—i.e., becomes the Superman or Purified Self. In "The Way of the Creative One," when Nietzsche remarks, "You yourself will always be the worst enemy you can meet," he is again referring to the lower, egotistical self. In the same chapter, "your way leads past yourself and your seven devils" is an uncanny divination of the seven stages of self and their "spirits of gravity" dragging one down, trying to arrest and reverse one's spiritual development, in Sufism.[60] "You must be ready to burn yourself in your own flame; how could you become new if you haven't first become ashes" is again the Phoenix-like rebirth of the self. And at the end of this chapter, "I love him who seeks to create beyond himself, and thus succumbs" is another reference to self-transcendence and the Superman, who is too similar in these respects to the Purified (or Perfected) Self in Sufism to be ignored.

Thus it appears as though Nietzsche has made undeniable progress in rediscovering the "Perfect Man" of Islamic Sufism. But he can never reach his goal, for he has already defeated his own purpose by positing that "God is dead." Hence he deprives his "higher species," the Superman or Overman (*übermensch*), of an ideal towards which to strive and approach asymptotically. The rocket he would shoot to the stars misfires and burrows into the ground: "'Man must become better and more evil'—thus do I teach. The most evil is necessary for the superman's best."[61] He castigates altruism as "the morality of decadence." "An 'altruistic' morality—one in which self-interest wilts away—remains a bad sign under all circumstances. . . . The best is lacking when self-interest begins to be lacking. . . . Man is finished when he becomes altruistic."[62] Approvingly calling his Zarathustra "the *destroyer* of morality"[63] and himself an "immoralist," he continues in *The Gay Science:* "You will never again pray, never again worship . . . you have no perpetual guardian and friend . . . there is no longer for you any rewarder and recompenser, no final corrector—there is no longer any reason in what happens, no longer any love in what happens to you. . . . "[64]

Thus, like Dr. Frankenstein, Nietzsche sets out to create a superior human being, yet succeeds only in producing a monster. In *Zarathustra,* he lets the cat out of the bag: "I guess you would call my overman—devil."[65] In *The Antichrist,* he defines happiness as "not peace, but war," and criticizes Christianity for having pictured "the strong man as the typically reprehensible man."[66] Barred from elevation in the vertical direction, his "self-overcoming" can take place in only one direction: the ego can only expand—or rather inflate—in the horizontal. Lacking this vertical direction, the only thing left for him is to claim superiority through his own will to power. Thus every individual is left pitted against every other, and a common morality becomes impossible. Locked in the basement of the Base Self, with evil and cruelty as its guides, with the only goal repudiated, with the elevator and even the stairway out of the labyrinth bricked over, his "superman" becomes not a sage or saint but a Hitler, a Stalin. His wine turns to vinegar, his elixir of life to poison. No wonder he went insane. As things stand, his "superman" is hopelessly confused—a hodgepodge of the highest stage of selfhood, the "Purified Self," and the worst of the Base Self—a tainted mixture instead of pure, clear, sparkling water.

Yet after all is said and done, it cannot be denied that Nietzsche had great potential in him. Had he fallen into the hands of a competent Master, he would no doubt have borne fruit, his mind and his spirit would have declared peace, and they would have begun to pull in the same direction instead of in opposite directions. Perhaps he himself might have become a "superman" in the better sense of the term. Nietzsche realized as much—"If only I had a Master!" he once exclaimed—but it was not to be. There was nothing in the Western intellectual tradition to provide Nietzsche with the master he needed, nor is there still.

The Base Self and Science

Let us now turn to the question of the Base Self versus knowledge. We have already noted that Nietzsche was a moralist of knowledge. Although he knew nothing about Sufism, he conceived of knowledge in two different ways: as sublime Truth (which Nietzsche attributed to Plato and the wisest of all ages), and as the subtlest guise of the Will to Power (which Nietzsche himself advocated: the will to truth is the Will to Power, the passion to rule). The first of these corresponds, in terms of Sufi psychology, to the Purified Self; the latter to the Base Self, the Ego.

Ever since Bacon, we have known that "knowledge is power." Lord Acton informed us that: "Power tends to corrupt and absolute power corrupts absolutely." Using the equivalence of knowledge and power, we arrive at: "absolute knowledge corrupts absolutely." This refers to the Base Self. The Base Self seeks knowledge not for its own sake, but for the love of power. This lust for power is progressively diminished as higher levels of selfhood are attained, until the Purified Self is reached; the latter contemplates knowledge as divine truth solely out of its love for Truth, not out of lust for the power that knowledge will give. Only the Purified Self is worthy of possessing knowledge, and deserves Truth, because it will never misappropriate, misuse, or abuse it.[67]

Hence, knowledge in the hands of the Base Self is extremely

dangerous. The more the selfish ego knows, the more arrogant does it become, the greater is its tendency to self-deification. And awareness of this fact has never been so relevant as it is today, in the Information Age of our scientific civilization. Never have we possessed so much knowledge, and never has science, or information, been so dangerously open to misuse.[68] Einstein's equation $E=mc^2$ is a case in point: from the knowledge that matter can be converted into energy, we have fashioned weapons that will destroy the human race. But Copernicus, at the very beginning of the scientific revolution, was already aware of the implications, which explains his reluctance to make his discoveries widely known.

The following apocryphal letter, purportedly by Lysis, shook Copernicus to his very core and caused him to withhold his great discoveries for almost four decades:

> After the death of Pythagoras . . . it remains our sacred duty to remember the divine teaching of our master and not to divulge the treasures of philosophy [read: "science"] to those who have not undergone preliminary purification of the mind. . . . Some of his imitators achieve many and great things, but in an improper way . . . thus their audience is encouraged to ruthlessness and insolence, for they stain the pure tenets of philosophy with rash and impure demeanour. It is as if one were to pour clean, fresh water into a well filled with dirt—for the dirt will only get agitated, and the water will be wasted. This is what happens to those who teach and are taught in this manner. Thick and dark forests cover the minds and hearts of those who have not been initiated in the proper manner, and disturb the mild contemplation of ideas. . . . [69]

The overtones of secrecy and initiation in the above go against the grain of our modern intellectual tradition, where knowledge is freely available and open to all who would avail themselves of it. Yet at the same time, we must realize that it contains a gem of truth: in the hands of the unwise, knowledge can, and does, lead to disaster. If knowledge is freely available to all, then all must also be endowed with the ethics to use it wisely. During the building of the atomic bomb, the scientists on the Manhattan Project were overcome by their curiosity and wonder: each technical hurdle became an exhilarating intellectual experience. With few exceptions (notably Leo Szilard), they gave little thought to the enormity of their achievements, to the uses to which their brainchild would finally be put.[70] Contrast this attitude with that of the great Christian physician Hunayn Ibn Ishaq (d. 873), who, when ordered to concoct a poison by the highest authorities, responded fearlessly: "I am skilled in useful things, and do not research other matters. My religion and my profession prevent me from this. My religion commands me to do good to other human beings, even if they are my enemies. As for my profession, it has been established for the happiness of the human race, and has forbidden harming our fellow men."

Yet once the atomic bomb was finished, the decision to use it, and to stockpile weapons the measure of whose destruction is beyond belief, was made by others. This signals the fact that in a technological civilization, *in a scientific society,*[71] *it is not enough to have scientists who are moral; everybody should pass through proper moral training.* And if one considers that university students can now design an atomic bomb, plus the fact that the smallest nations are eager to lay hands on one, it becomes clear that the project must be worldwide.

All this demonstrates that in order to handle knowledge wisely, we must aim at an elevation and purification of the Base Self. But this is precisely the project of Islamic Sufism, which envisions the training and purification of the Self through seven successive stages, beginning with the Base (or Egotistical) Self and ending with the Purified Self. Ideally, only the Purified Self has the right to higher knowledge (whether physical or spiritual), for only it can wield and use such knowledge selflessly, with wisdom and compassion. Otherwise, knowledge or information in the hands of the Base Self can only lead to the misuse and abuse of power. Scientists, if they are not themselves evil, then become the instruments of those who are. In his novel *Ape and Essence,* Aldous Huxley portrayed this graphically by representing Einstein at the end of a leash held by a gorilla in a general's uniform.

This should not be misunderstood as a call to elitism. It is a call to the *democratization of self-purification,* somewhat in the manner of general education. This was what Islamic societies in general, and Ottoman society in particular, attempted at their zenith—the institutions of formal education (the *madrasahs*) were complemented by informal schools giving spiritual training (the Sufi *takkas*)—although the world of Islam could not finally maintain its superior stand, because physical knowledge fell into unwise and undeserved neglect. The exquisite balance between physical and spiritual knowledge was lost—*just as we have today lost the same balance,* this time at the expense of spiritual knowledge. What we now have to do is revive this vision—to consider the increase of knowledge together with the increase in morality and concomitant levels of selfhood needed to use that knowledge wisely, humanely, life-affirmatively. If our spiritual and moral progress does not match our scientific progress, all will sooner or later be lost, as would be the case with a bunch of irresponsible children playing with matches in a warehouse full of dynamite.

The Question of Darwinism

While dealing with the subject of science, let us briefly consider the case of Darwin. Science—which has improved our lives to such a phenomenal extent—also places a dilemma before us. To put it simply, science had to provide an answer to the question "Where did all this come from?" It had to provide a convincing explanation for all the "signs" in the world—its interconnectivity, its grandeur, its sheer beauty—all of which point dangerously to "Meaning." It had to provide an alternative explanation of the universe, without reference to a Creator. And this was primarily achieved by Darwin.

If Nietzsche was the *enfant terrible* of nineteenth-century philosophy, Darwin represents the corresponding legacy of that century's science. One hesitates to criticize Darwin, that soft-spoken, civilized man, that great student of nature. And of course, what is scientific in his studies must always remain above reproach.

What Darwin demonstrated beyond the shadow of a doubt was *adaptation*: the fact that individual species exhibit great resilience in conforming to the demands of nature. Light speckled moths become dark speckled moths, etc. Yet there must be a limit to this elasticity, otherwise a species would simply mutate into another species instead of becoming extinct. Such a species-metamorphosis (macroevolution) has often been claimed, but never satisfactorily demonstrated.

It is not in Darwin's science that the problem resides, then, but in the unstated metaphysical assumptions which underlie his more speculative assertions. These metaphysical presuppositions, after they have been planted and have gestated for a sufficient period, resurface in the mindset that Darwinian concepts of evolution configure. Here, for instance, is William Provine, Professor of Biological Sciences at Cornell University: "Our modern understanding of evolution implies . . . that ultimate meaning in life is nonexistent."[72] Or behold Richard Dawkins, a leading Darwinian proponent, operating in the Nietzsche mode: "The universe we observe has precisely the properties we should expect if there is, at bottom, no design, no purpose, no evil and no good, nothing but blind, pitiless indifference. . . . But what I want to guard against is people therefore getting nihilistic in their personal lives. I don't see any reason for that at all. You can have a very happy and fulfilled personal life even if you think [as Dawkins admits he does] that the universe at large is a tale told by an idiot ["full of sound and fury, signifying nothing"— Shakespeare]. You can still set up goals and have a very worthwhile life and not be nihilistic about it at a personal level."[73] Hence Provine is not alone in his interpretation.

Two things are noteworthy about Dawkins' views. The first is that the universe does not "have" these properties. Rather, it conforms to our expectations about it, or we select those aspects of it that fit our presuppositions and disregard the rest. Whenever a supposedly scientific theory—which should be confining its scope to the biology on this dust speck known as Earth—results in sweeping, unfalsifiable, philosophical generalizations about the nature of the cosmos at large, we would do well to remain on our guard, a point that Dawkins unwittingly concedes when he says a little further on that "I think it is not helpful to apply Darwinian language too widely." I'll take my metaphysics without chili pepper, thank you.

The second is that Dawkins correctly identifies the end result of this line of thought: nihilism. And it is here, if anywhere, that the effects of Darwin and Nietzsche on the human mind coincide. But he is mistaken in thinking that everyone can survive such a philosophy intact. Brave souls such as Dawkins or Bertrand Russell might stoically face the fact that, to paraphrase the latter, "blind, omnipotent matter rolls its relentless way," but ordinary mortals are incapable of such a feat.

Being brave and stoic, moreover, is not sufficient proof that the views of a person possessing such noble attributes happen to be true. Why suffer the shattering implications of a nihilistic philosophy if it is patently false to begin with? The fatal error occurs when, like Hume and Nietzsche before them, the advocates of Darwinian evolution elevate chance to the status of a god. Thus Jacques Monod: "Chance alone is at the source of every innovation, of all creation in the biosphere. Pure chance, absolutely free but blind, is at the very root of the stupendous edifice of creation."[74]

Yet the very word "chance" subtly imposes on us a value judgment about the cosmos: it implies that things can occur in this universe *without any reason at all*. Small wonder, then, that Darwin's disciples harvest meaninglessness from his concepts: they have not reaped anything more than what was sown in the first place. (The mathematical implausibility, if not impossibility, of random evolution lies beyond the scope of this book; the interested reader is referred to the writings of mathematician David Berlinski.[75] Suffice it to say that it takes the universe a veritable eternity just to construct a single biological molecule by chance.)

Charles Darwin himself was not immune to the nihilistic acid of his theory. Before the great turning point of his life, he had been a devout man, and on at least one occasion, watching the grandeur of the Brazilian forest, he had a religious, "deep inward experience" which left him convinced that there must be more to man than "the mere breath of his body."

But then came the Galapagos Islands, *The Origin of Species* (1859), and the theory of evolution by random mutation and natural selection. The first of these concepts is probabilistic, the second entirely deterministic, so that the conceptual symmetry has a certain philosophical appeal. The following picture might be helpful: one scoops up an armful of tennis balls and hurls them haphazardly at a grating, some of which pass through while others, naturally enough, don't.

The problem with the Darwinian theory is that it is a purely *mechanistic* theory: it removes not only the necessity of a Creator (though without explaining the question of who designed the machine in the first place), but also the concept of any *purpose* in nature. (One should call this probabilistic mechanism: nature was reduced to a giant pinball machine, a random number generator.) As for human beings, they were reduced to soulless robots. Thus does one progress from Descartes, who thought of animals as machines, through La Mettrie's *Man a Machine* (1747) a century later, to the widespread acceptance of this insidious idea thanks to Darwinian metaphysics. "I have loved my fellow men," wrote D. H. Lawrence in his *Last Poems,* "and lived to learn that they are neither fellow nor men but machine robots." And once this basic ingredient, this jaundiced world view, is in place, the "robot state" or insect society, depending on what you want to call it, cannot be far behind—as evidenced in the robot states of the twentieth century.

Generations fed on evolutionary theory were overcome by a sense of emptiness and purposelessness in life—not least, Darwin himself. He felt as if he were a man who had become color-blind. During the same critical period as his scientific achievements, when he was about thirty, Darwin suffered what he himself called a "curious and lamentable loss of the higher aesthetic tastes." Like Sartre's Roquentin, an attempt to re-read Shakespeare bored him "to the point of physical nausea." In his autobiography he complained that he had formerly been fond of poetry:

> But now for many years I cannot endure to read a line of poetry. My mind seems to have become a kind of machine for grinding general laws out of a large collection of facts, but why this should have caused the atrophy of that part of the brain on which the higher tastes depend, I cannot conceive. The loss of these tastes is a loss of happiness, and may possibly be injurious to the intellect, and more probably to the moral character, by enfeebling the emotional part of our nature.[76]

We should be careful here to distinguish Darwin from the more strident of his followers. The son of an atheistic father, he himself never went that far. Though a self-confessed agnostic in his later years, he also said: "I have never been an Atheist in the sense of denying the existence of a God." ("Darwin," says Dawkins concerning his followers, "made it possible to be an intellectually fulfilled atheist.") But because his mind conceived of all nature, all life forms, and even all human beings as machines, it was visited by a taste of its own medicine: it turned into a machine itself.

A machine cannot feel; if animals and human beings are robots, then what we call "feelings" are merely epiphenomena that can be disregarded, they do not really exist. What a convenient excuse for vivisectionists, for torturers. What a whopping encouragement for the despots of past and future concentration camps. What a whitewash for their blood-drenched consciences. And I have not even brought in "nature red in tooth and claw" yet.

Let me repeat, before some people get entirely lost, that the scientific achievements of Darwin are not themselves in doubt. Nor is there any doubt that the world cannot have started at the date 4004 B.C. The real issues are only clouded and obscured by such chaff. Nor does all this mean that evolution itself need necessarily be discarded, as long as we realize that this has to be guided or directed evolution.[77] What is possible is that one phase of nonrandom behavior crystallizes into another phase of nonrandom behavior—the ordinary laws of probability are suspended, and another level of determinism begins to operate.

A student of Sufism would be tempted to conjecture that, since man is the all-comprehensive life form, the genomes of all other organisms are subsets of the human genome, and that an information- and organization-based approach will prove much more fruitful in the future than a temporal-evolutionary one. But I wish to avoid speculation. Whether this is true or not will emerge in due time, given the spectacular advances in gene sequencing.

The Consequences

So much for the beginning—but what of the end? What are the final consequences of the loss of belief in God? Nietzsche's formula cost him his sanity; what is the outcome if large sections of humanity cease to believe in God?

It is no longer possible to ignore the following fact: highfalutin, abstract metaphysical propositions *have consequences in the physical world.* A philosophical proposition declaimed by a pundit from his ivory tower, when acclaimed and acted out by men of lesser intelligence and even less conscience, leads to concrete results in the real world. These are the fruits of that seed, and "by their fruits you shall judge them." The fruits immediately lay bare the peculiar properties concealed in the seed, which cannot be discovered without sowing it.

Nietzsche's formula has been sown for more than a century. It has become a standard, a stock item, an integral part in the intellectual equipment of the West. During this time, it has had the chance to grow, to bear fruit. A century after Nietzsche, where do we find ourselves?

The history of the twentieth century has been one of increasing decimation and devastation. The discovery of the most hideous weapon in history at the end of World War II has guaranteed that there will be few, if any, survivors at the end of the next world war, and those few will envy the dead. Two bombs—two bombs were all we had in 1945. Today we have not ten, not one hundred, but *tens of thousands* of these weapons, temporarily gathering mothballs. But don't be fooled—they're still there, all nations are lusting after them, and there's enough raw material for thousands more. The H-Bombs in their cocoons, the ballistic missiles in their silos may be hibernating now, but when their springtime comes they will resume proliferation.

Alongside this tremendous increase in murder-power—and murder is its proper name, for their greatest destruction is wrought on innocent civilians—the twentieth century has witnessed atrocities unparalleled in history. Human beings have slaughtered each other in gas chambers, in ovens, in concentration camps, under torture, not by the thousands but by the *tens of millions*. To paraphrase Turkish poet M. A. Ersoy, "whole continents went boiling down into that maelstrom."[78]

What is the magnitude of the death toll? Precise figures are impossible to obtain. In a chapter on "The Century of Megadeath" in his *Out of Control* (1993), Zbigniew Brzezinski attempted a rough estimate. His reckoning is conservative, and closer to a minimum value than what the losses actually were.

Brzezinski estimated that approximately 87 million people perished in wars during the twentieth century. More than 80 million were murdered in cold blood as a result of ideologically motivated terror and totalitarian genocide. Thus upwards of 167 million, or almost 170 million people, represent the lower limit on this century's dreadful ledger. "This," concludes Brzezinski, "is more than the total killed in all previous wars, civil conflicts, and religious persecutions throughout human history."[79] Add to this the number of dead in regional conflicts since the end of the Cold War,[80] 90 percent of whom were civilians, and the turn-of-the-century figure is sure to exceed the 200 million mark. The mind cannot deal adequately with carnage of such monstrous proportions and is numbed into incomprehension by the very magnitudes involved. This incomprehension serves as a refuge for the human mind, which instinctively recoils from coming to terms with evil of such dimensions.

The 70 million dead in two world wars; the 50 million dead or missing in combat during the so-called "peace" period since the last world war; the 6 million Jews butchered in extermination camps; the untold millions handed over to famine; the tens of millions who perished in the Soviet Gulag (the devastation is of such magnitude that accurate figures cannot be cited, estimates ranging between 15 and 66 million); the comparable number who went to their deaths in China[81]; the progressive institutionalization of torture by almost all the nations of the world; the ever-increasing degree of violence in the *methods* of torture; the lack of compassion for women, children, and the aged—quite to the contrary, the compulsion to inflict even more merciless torture on precisely those who are most at our mercy[82]—the terrors of the twentieth century are far beyond those of any horror movie. What has happened in *fact* leaves *fiction* speechless, no matter how depraved or imaginative. George Steiner hit the nail on the head:

> The concentration and death camps of the twentieth century, wherever they exist, under whatever régime, are *Hell made immanent*. They are the transference of Hell from below the earth to its surface. . . . The absence of the familiar damned opened a vortex which the modern totalitarian state has filled.[83]

It is crucially important that we understand the reason for this. Why should it happen? What is going on? The reason is that without belief in God, or the proper exercise of morality and self-purification, there is nothing to hold the Base Self in check. Fear and love of God cannot exist unless you have belief in Him first. Fear of God restrains the Base Self, preventing it from descending too far towards the negative. Love of God elevates the self towards the positive (i.e., God and Heaven). When belief in God is eliminated, therefore, the push from below (fear) and the pull from above (love) collapse with it, and the elevator plummets under the gravitational pull of Hell. The ego unleashed then becomes a conduit, a volcanic shaft, through which infernal contents erupt into everyday life. Under certain conditions—of which the paramount is lack of faith in God—the Base Self becomes truly satanic: a mere plaything, a puppet, of Satan. It makes no difference that a person under this influence remains unaware of his situation, all the while denying the existence of God, Satan, Heaven and Hell—his very denial makes him all the more susceptible to this generally unrecognized law of human nature.

True, men have always practiced cruelty. But it is in the *degree* and *scale* of cruelty that the last century has surpassed all others. Previously, religions held man's selfish drives in check and counseled compassion for all of "God's little creatures." A true Moslem, for instance, would empathize with Abu Bakr, who said: "My Lord, put me in your Hell and expand me to its limits, so that no place will be left for the suffering of anyone else." Thus whereas in the past the majority of humanity had compassion even for animals—whereas they would try to spare even an ant, an insect, from being trampled over—we now stockpile weapons to decimate *our very own children*. And *this* is the concrete result of loss of belief in God. Without that faith, morality cannot exist, and still less can it be practiced properly. Nietzsche's premonitions, quoted at the beginning of this paper, have been realized with a vengeance. It is no accident that the same person who foretold the death of belief in God also was intelligent enough to foresee its consequences.

Is God to blame for all this? Is there a single divine commandment that orders us to do this? Since when has "Thou shalt not kill" been inverted into "Thou shalt"? Or is it rather that our own selfish egos have performed the inversion?

It is not God who desires it this way. God has placed us on this Earth as its stewards, not to maltreat each other and other creatures. If we abide by His laws, we should live in harmony with Him, with ourselves, with one another, with nature, and with all creation. If we do not, things will get progressively worse, and finally we shall *burn down the Earth*—we shall incinerate it to a cinder. We shall collectively become *murderers of our own children. It is not God,* but our egotistical selves, that will dictate this outcome. He who forgets God cannot recognize his children, either.

To see how much our destructive activities run at cross-purposes to God, we need only look at why He created the universe in the first place. This is a separate matter, to be dealt with at length in Chapter 2.

The Search for Superman

Perhaps, in Nietzsche's time, the consequences of disbelief were still not sufficiently apparent. Perhaps it could still be claimed that a metaphysical belief was no different from the lack thereof. But today, we do not have this luxury open to us. Everything is now crystal clear. Man at the pinnacle of civilization, science, and technology can be said to be no different than a caveman wearing a tie. In terms of his *capacity* to inflict destruction, he is much worse.

"Hatred does not cease by hatred; hatred ceases by love." Such is the teaching of all true religions. The heart of all religion is love. We cannot extinguish fire with fire. To douse fire, water is required—the water of peace, the water of life. Belief in God, and meticulous performance of His requirements for humanity, constitute this water.

If belief in God is dead, then Doomsday is on the agenda. Mankind will self-destruct sooner or later in a gigantic spasm of insanity. Disbelief in God, in short, can mean only one thing: man's collective suicide. Nietzsche gives voice to a "deepest suspicion that is more and more gaining worse and worse control of us Europeans and that could easily confront coming generations with the terrifying Either/Or: 'Either abolish your reverences or—yourselves!' The latter would be nihilism; but would not the former also be—nihilism? That is *our* question mark."[84]

In retrospect, we can see that the question is not one of Either/Or, but Both/And—better yet, If/Then: *If* you abolish faith in God, *then* you abolish yourselves. The first nihilism begets the second.

In *The Twilight of the Idols,* Nietzsche makes the following uncanny observation: "We have abolished the true world [the ideal world of Plato, the God of Christian religion]: which world is left? Perhaps the apparent one? Certainly not! Together with the true world we have also abolished the apparent one!"[85] Nietzsche here makes the distinction between Necessary Being (God) and Contingent Being (universe) as dealt with in Sufism and Islamic philosophy, predicating the existence of the latter on the "Ground of all being." Much more eerily and perhaps unwittingly, he shows that by shutting the door on the light of God, we cripple the projection of that light into the universe. For the heart of a mystic or saint is a doorway to God's light, an avenue through which love and mercy shine into the world. The more friends of God there are, the closer we are to the Kingdom of Heaven. But so long as that door remains closed, peace, love, and meaning are not replenished but depleted, and mankind becomes steadily more depraved, merciless, and desperate—psychologically abnormal. The stage grows darker and darker, until mankind's collective consciousness of the universe is blotted out in a catastrophic paroxysm of global proportions.

If Nietzsche is the prophet of atheism, *Thus Spoke Zarathustra* is the Bible of atheism. But one fundamental question remains: why, then, was Nietzsche not content with the simple death of God; why did he find it necessary to search beyond it for Zarathustra and the Superman? The reason is that *he cannot stop,* and man cannot stop; his noble spirit, though choking, continues on its spiritual quest. Nietzsche's greatness resides in the fact that he realizes that something higher, something greater, lies beyond his conceptions, even if he cannot come to proper terms with it. His attempt manifests itself, as Jung demonstrates, in the archetypal symbol of Zarathustra. Nietzsche is trying to find a way out of the nihilism that the death of God leaves in its wake. In the best humanistic tradition, he devalues a God "out there" in order to elevate Man. But what if God is not merely external to man, but also internal to him?[86]

By rejecting God *in toto,* Nietzsche also inadvertently devalues man. Man is thereby estranged from the divine spark within and left as a husk, a mere shell. He is alienated from the wellsprings of his soul. In *The Gay Science,* Nietzsche proposes that man should not *flow out* to a God, but should ever accumulate water like a dam; he fails to see that it is the same God who *flows into* man, nourishing him from within, so that if man builds a dam against God, he will be left in the end with a dry riverbed on both sides of the dam, for the spring will dry up—or rather, be diverted. Nietzsche thus obviates any possibility of man's self-realization and defeats the purpose of his mission. But man as he exists now is an unfinished being and will always try to transcend himself; atheist or not, this is the human condition.

The quest that Nietzsche set out on has been realized in all true spiritual traditions, of which Islamic Sufism represents the culmination. From his *Birth of Tragedy* to the very end, this is the tragedy of Nietzsche, and this tragedy has become part of the very fabric of the twentieth century. "The true calling of man," said Aldous Huxley echoing Nietzsche, "is to find the way to himself." The "death of God" has blighted our lives to the extent that it has become the definitive concept in modern thought, and it is high time—"the highest time," in Zarathustra's words—that we began the examination of Sufism in this light.

Nietzsche criticized Christianity for its supernatural aspect, for its emphasis on spirit to the detriment of nature, for its denial of nature and worldly life; and he was genius enough to see where this dichotomy has been transcended: "the culture of *Islam* . . . more congenial to our senses and tastes than Rome and Greece . . . owed its origins to noble . . . instincts, because it said Yes to life. . . . "[87] He saw, in other words, that the pairs of opposites (God/man, body/spirit, good/bad, etc.) are here constellated in a radically different way, and that the rights of the body are recognized just as much as the rights of the spirit. A little more time, and he might also have realized that the "transvaluation of values" he was searching for had been—or could be—effected only in Islam. For at bottom he was trying not to do away with all values, but to transcend conventional morality with all its mendacity, contradictions, and hypocrisies, to go beyond the specifically *Christian* conceptions of good and evil; and "evil" in the Christian sense has never existed in Islam.

"Nietzsche was by no means anti-moral in general but only anti-moral in the Christian, Buddhist, or any other strength-denying senses. He wanted to go beyond Good and Evil to reach the valid (as he thought) opposition, Good and Bad"[88]—which are precisely the categories found in Islam.[89] In line with the ego/power relationship discussed in this chapter, he attempted to formulate the contents of these ethical categories solely in terms of power[90]; but in addition to that, a sick, ailing, sleepless ex-professor, in pain but also in love with life, can perhaps be excused his resentment for weakness in all its forms; it is his own weaknesses he is reacting against. To him, life is strength; hence his opposition to Buddhism no less than to Christianity, as well as all other life-denying religions that wish to escape this world.[91]

The Nightmare of Insanity

Nietzsche, who said "God is dead," finally went insane. In a premonitory nightmare attributed to Zarathustra, Nietzsche provides us with a rare and chilling glimpse into his condition.

> I had turned my back on all life, thus I dreamed. I had become a night watchman and a guardian of tombs upon the lonely mountain castle of Death. Up there I guarded his coffins. . . . Life that had been overcome looked at me out of glass coffins. I breathed the odor of dusty eternities: sultry and dusty lay my soul. And who could have aired his soul there?
>
> The brightness of midnight was always about me; loneliness crouched next to it; and as a third, death-rattle silence, the worst of my friends. I had keys, the rustiest of all keys; and I knew how to use them to open the most creaking of all gates. Like a wickedly angry croaking, the sound ran through the long corridors when the gate's wings moved: fiendishly cried this bird, ferocious at being awakened. Yet still more terrible and heart-constricting was the moment when silence returned and it grew quiet about me, and I sat alone in this treacherous silence.
>
> Thus time passed and crawled, if time still existed. . . . But eventually that happened which awakened me. Thrice, strokes struck at the gate like thunder; the vaults echoed and howled thrice; then I went to the gate. "Alpa," I cried, "who is carrying his ashes up the mountain? Alpa! Alpa! Who is carrying his ashes up the mountain?"[92] And I pressed the key and tried to lift the gate and exerted myself; but still it did not give an inch. Then a roaring wind tore its wings apart; whistling, shrilling, and piercing, it cast up a black coffin before me.

And amid the roaring and whistling and shrilling the coffin burst and spewed out a thousandfold laughter. And from a thousand grimaces of children, angels, owls, fools, and butterflies as big as children, it laughed and mocked and roared at me. Then I was terribly frightened; it threw me to the ground. And I cried in horror as I have never cried. And my own cry awakened me—and I came to my senses.[93]

As Professor Jung points out in his masterly analysis of this dream: "It is a horrible foreboding of [Nietzsche's] insanity. . . . Insanity is the secret, the utter destruction of his mind. . . . [The dream is weakly attributed to Zarathustra's "enemies."] But who is his enemy? His own unconscious—his enemy is himself. So he has dreamt himself, that is his own case, his own insanity."[94]

Having identified "God" with death and the devil in his mind, Nietzsche's dream takes the form of a descent into Hades, into hell. From time immemorial men have tried to master the unconscious—to unlock its secrets and to dominate it—using the rusty keys of their willpower. But the unconscious has always proved singularly impervious to such attempts at taming it: it has a life, a will of its own, and the will to power is ineffectual against it.

Nietzsche's Abysmal Thought, his unconscious, asks a question which Nietzsche reiterates above: "Who is carrying his own ashes up the mountain?" The answer is: Nietzsche himself is carrying the ashes of his own burnt-out mind. And the black coffin—both blackness and coffin symbolizing death—is again Nietzsche, out of which issues the thousand peals of laughter, the insane laughter of Nietzsche. (Zarathustra's disciple recognizes as much: "Are you not yourself the coffin?" he asks.) He tries to unlock the creaky gates of his unconscious; but his unconscious is also straining at the gates from the other side,[95] and it then

bursts forth with a roar, sweeping away the thin fabric of his reason, inundating him, overwhelming him with its contents—
which is indeed what happened in the end. He became one of the
"undead": a dead mind in a living body, an insane laughter in a
coffin.

Such a welling up of the unconscious—whether spontaneous
or drug-induced—leaves one as helpless as a small boat on
stormy seas. Under these conditions, there is only one solution:
to anchor oneself solidly to the ground of this ocean—the
Ground of all Being who is also the Ground of the unconscious.
God, and God alone, can help against this merciless onslaught,
and by taking refuge in God, by fixing one's attention, centering
one's thoughts on God,[96] one can be saved from drowning
before the storm abates. But if we have repudiated God like
Nietzsche, then there is nothing solid left to hold on to, and then
there is "no exit" from the hell of insanity: certainly Nietzsche,
who considered his Zarathustra—and therefore himself—as "a
psychologist . . . who has no equal,"[97] did not prove immune.

To the extent that we think God is dead, we partake of
Nietzsche's madness, we participate—however partially or subconsciously—in his insanity. In these relatively halcyon days, we
cannot perceive that danger lurks just beyond the horizon. The
subconscious contents of the collectivity of psyches is, however,
there as always—unless and until we put our inner house in
order, until we actively resolve ourselves. Therefore, if we wish
to avoid this fate, if we wish to avoid the precipice towards
which we all are still invisibly hurtling, we would do well to heed
the following wise words:

He whose footsteps you follow in,
His destination you will reach.

This chapter has traced a path that leads to "hell"—the nature and the consequences of Nietzsche's rejection of all kinds of law; the deification of chance; and misconceptions about man (as god) and God (as a tyrant—we observed at this point that God conforms to our vision of Him). We introduced a key concept for this book—the Base Self—and suggested that instead of a culture under its control, we stand in need of a "democratization of self-purification." Chapter 2 now offers an explanation of God's true purpose for man.

2

THE UNIVERSE, ENLIGHTENMENT, AND ETHICS

*You do not venture beyond the house of Nature. How
can you expect to reach the neighborhood of Reality?*
—KHWAJA HAFIZ

Man and Universe

The scale on which the pageant of the universe unfolds is awesome. We are not even specks on Earth, the Earth is not even a speck in the Milky Way, and our galaxy is not even a speck among the countless other galaxies in the universe. Compared with the age of the Earth, estimated at about five billion years, the entire history of the human race is but a brief flicker. Since the sun itself is expected to shine for another five billion years, man stands practically at the nexus between past eternity and future eternity in terms of time, and between minus and plus infinity in terms of space.

Man is not even a dot in terms of cosmic space, and he is not even the blink of an eye in cosmic time. This picture of the universe would crush man to nothingness, would annihilate him instantly, were it not for the following subtle fact:

Outer than the outermost, inner than the innermost, beyond the beyond, within the within, is God Almighty, Lord of the universe, Lord of all the worlds.[98] Like a deep-sea fish whose inner pressure prevents it from being crushed by the tremendous pressure of the ocean depths, faith in God saves man from despair and lends him the resistance needed to withstand the vicissitudes of life. If he is connected to God, if he is rooted in the Almighty, man can draw on an unlimited supply of inner strength and fortitude, rescuing him from nihilism and self-destruction.

This marvelous universe is the home of man, who is no alien to it but was designed into it from the start. "I and the ten thousand things," remarked the Chinese sage Chuang Tzu, "came into being together." No less than the stellar phenomena trillions of times our size yet which we can barely see, we too are part of the design of the universe. The same intricate blueprints that laid down the plans of the galaxies or the atomic nucleus went into designing human DNA. It was *all at once*. Just as a playwright can entertain different sections of a play—or even entire plays—simultaneously in his mind, God is capable of casting past, present and future in a single timeless instant. Everything— cosmological constants and all—had to be planned down to the minutest detail. In a probabilistic universe, there are so many things that can go wrong that God had to make sure at the very beginning that man would be the outcome (this is known as the "strong anthropic principle" in science).

Man is suspended between the infinitely large and the infinitely small—at a point of inflection, so to speak. This center position allows man to probe and comprehend both a macrocosmos of galactic superclusters and a microcosmos of elementary particles.

What is more, all ancient traditions have agreed that *man is* not a nonentity, but the noblest of God's creations, a cosmos in miniature—*a microcosm*.

This man is not *any* man, however, whom you may choose to pick off the streets. The traditions of India, of China, of Hermeticism, of Islamic Sufism, all speak of the Whole Man, the Perfect Man, the King, the True Man, the Primordial Man (Adam Kadmon), the Viceregent of God on Earth. But every human being partakes of this honor by belonging to the same species, to the extent that s/he shares the attributes of the Universal Human. It is for this reason that "the world has been placed at your disposal," as God informs the human race in the Book.

The ancient traditions are unanimous in telling us that somehow, in some unfathomable sense, this human being is homologous with the universe; the universe is mapped into man.[99] A saying attributed to Hermes Trismegistus states: "The world is a living creature endowed with a body which men can see and an intelligence which men cannot see."[100] A Sufi expressed it even more clearly: "Truth/God is the life and soul of the universe, and the whole universe is His body." Another Sufi sage wrote the following couplet:

The universe is a great book of God from end to end;
Whichever letter you check, the meaning always
comes out "God."

One is reminded here of the claim, repeated by both the Bible and Mohammed, that God created man in His own image. This too is incomprehensible to us, but if, as the sources of Sufism tell us, "the universe is man writ large, man is cosmos in the small," then the "macroman" or "ultra-man"[101] would be such a being that an entire galaxy would be merely a hair on its body, or a cell in it.

One thing is certain: the external description of the universe can only be a starting point for unraveling its mysteries. "The universe has remained beyond comprehension," notes Hans Koning, "even if we are now able to count the number of electrons it holds. . . . "[102] The zillions or the zillionths that we can measure are only the wrappings of a gift that is as inscrutable as it is wonderful—the gift of being human in this vast, amazing universe.

The Significance of Man

The story of the creation of the universe has been painstakingly pieced together by scientists on the basis of physical observations. Despite the grandeur of that vision, it is still incomplete, because it is based on monocular or "single vision"—it does not take into account that component of the universe called "spiritual" and hence is too constricted. The following description is offered with the hope that scientists will be able to discover and elaborate on its mathematical and physical dimensions as well.[103]

When God decided to create the universe, He began by "defining" Permanent Archetypes (or Immutable Essences)[104] and positing Names and Attributes through which divine light shone. These may be compared to a system of lenses and prisms that ordinary white light passes through, resulting in an endless, ever-changing rainbow interplay of patterns and colors. This last corresponds, in our analogy, to the created universe.

The following mathematical metaphor ("mathephor"?) may be helpful. First, there is Nonspace ("the space of spaces," in Sheikh Geylani's words). From this is spawned an infinite-dimensional superspace filled with infinite energy or potential (it is a plenum, not a vacuum). In this space, certain abstract, multidimensional reference points are defined for its decomposition or differentiation into subspaces with differing qualitative characteristics. It is the intersection of two or more of these subspaces that gives rise either to the prototypes of entities existing in the observable universe, or to the entities themselves.

Thus, any given creature is connected to one or more Permanent Archetypes and is a locus of manifestation for one or more Divine Attributes and Names. Physical size or temporal extensity is of little importance here; what matters is complexity. The human brain may be incomparably smaller than a galaxy, but it is the most marvelously complex piece of organic matter in the universe.

Not the brain alone, however, but the total human constitution is the purpose of creation. The reason is that, while all other things in the universe are loci of manifestation for some—perhaps many—Names and Attributes, only the constitution of a human being, including his spiritual dimension, has the capacity to manifest *all* of them.[105]

God has infinitely many Attributes, which become manifest in the creation of the universe, and His Names are the names of these Attributes. "God made man in His own image" means that God made man in His Attributes—*all* of them. This is why, despite his insignificance in cosmic terms, man is the acme of creation and the intent behind it. The human being who has realized this potential is the one whom we call Archetypal, Cosmic, or Perfect. If we obey His commandments and follow His instructions to the letter, this is what God has in store for us; but even partial success will be amply rewarded. The Universal Man has become a "cosmos in miniature" in the sense that his essential attributes are arranged—constellated—in the same structure and composition as the Attributes that give birth to the universe—a possibility that the humanists, for all their exaltation of man, never dared to think about even in their wildest dreams.

In one respect, there is something disturbing about this parallelism between man and universe. When we look at the organic matter that composes him, and then at the cosmos, there seems to be no correlation whatever between the two. How do we reconcile them?

Think of the fruit of a particular tree. The fruit does not resemble the tree at all, yet we know that the DNA coded into the fruit is capable of representing—and reproducing—the entire tree. Hence, the lack of similarity between the tree and its fruit does not invalidate the claim that the fruit contains the essence of the tree.

In a similar way, man is the fruit of the cosmos. He has grown out of it as its most delicate, refined product, and if it is properly cultivated, it has the potential to grow into the cosmos. But just as man can represent the universe, he can also remain stuck at a partial representation, or can represent the baser aspects of the universe. From the heart of the Complete Man, however, the entire universe can flower.

So why did God create the universe? According to the Sufis, here is the answer. God said: "I created the universe for man, and man I created for myself." Again, in a vision of Geylani, He has stated: "I am man's secret, and man is my secret."

Once, a question was asked in the presence of the Master: What was God doing during the three billion years of life on Earth before the appearance of humanity? He answered: "Decorating the Earth for man."

All this goes to show that man is the most essential part of the universe. For this reason, the destruction of humankind cannot be the purpose of God, although it is within the realm of the possible. The Master used to quote what is a Sacred Tradition according to Sufi lore: "We will not destroy humankind, they will destroy themselves." God did not wait fifteen billion years just to see His handiwork annihilated, and if that had been His intention, He could have chosen not to create humanity in the first place.

Let us now investigate the ethics/enlightenment connection.

Whatever You Do Comes Back to You

God created the universe in a way mysterious to us, but not to the Sufis. For in creating each being, He placed a divine spark from Himself into its core. God, who is our Source and at our very spiritual center, is also at the heart of everything else.

This means that if you maltreat another, you are mistreating the divine spark, and through that creature offending the very God you are in search of.

Because the God at its center is no different from the God at your center, your action, whether good or ill, will bounce back. Perhaps not immediately. But within the intricate workings of the universe, sooner or later. This is an inexorable principle, an immutable law.

Whatever you do, you do to yourself.
Let me illustrate this by a Sufi teaching-story.

THERE WAS ONCE A MADMAN OF GOD, A *majzub*.[106] HE WAS ALWAYS WANDERING ABOUT TOWN, CALLING OUT: "WHATEVER YOU DO, YOU DO TO YOURSELF." HE USED TO PASS BENEATH THE WINDOWSILL OF A PARTICULAR WOMAN, AND IT WAS VERY DISTURBING TO HER TO HEAR THESE WORDS REPEATED ALL THE TIME. SLOWLY A RESENTMENT GREW IN HER, WHICH BY AND BY TURNED INTO AN ICY RESOLVE. "I'M GOING TO HAVE DONE WITH THIS MADMAN ONCE AND FOR ALL," SHE SAID TO HERSELF.

SHE BAKED A LOAF OF BREAD, DOSING IT WITH A LIBERAL AMOUNT OF POISON, AND WHEN THE MADMAN WAS PASSING UNDER HER WINDOW AGAIN, SHE CALLED OUT TO HIM.

PUTTING ON HER MOST DISARMING SMILE, SHE SAID, "MY GOOD MAN, YOU MUST BE HUNGRY. HERE IS A FRESHLY BAKED LOAF OF BREAD FOR YOU." AND SHE GAVE HIM THE BREAD.

THE MADMAN LOOKED AT HER AND SAID, "WHATEVER YOU DO, YOU DO TO YOURSELF," FOR HE NEVER SAID ANYTHING ELSE. HE TOOK THE BREAD AND WANDERED OFF.

WHEN HE CAME TO THE OUTSKIRTS OF THE CITY WHERE A CEMETERY WAS, HE WENT INTO THE CEMETERY, LAID THE BREAD ON THE LOW WALL OF THE CEMETERY, LAY DOWN, AND FELL ASLEEP.

THE WOMAN'S SON HAD BEEN AWAY FOR A LONG TIME AND WAS RETURNING HOME JUST THEN. HE HAD FINISHED HIS MILITARY DUTY. AS HE PASSED THE CEMETERY, HE SAW A LOAF OF BREAD ON THE WALLTOP. HE WAS FAMISHED. HE LOOKED AROUND TO SEE WHETHER THE BREAD HAD AN OWNER. HE COULD SEE NO ONE, SO, ASSUMING THAT THE BREAD HAD SOMEHOW BEEN ABANDONED, HE TOOK THE BREAD AND ATE IT.

A SHORT WHILE LATER, THE POISON BEGAN TO TAKE EFFECT. THE YOUNG MAN DIED IN AGONY. PASSERS-BY FOUND HIM AND, RECOGNIZING WHO HE WAS, MOURNFULLY TOOK HIM HOME TO HIS MOTHER. AS SHE WAS WAILING IN ANGUISH, THE SOUND OF THE MADMAN, WHO HAD AWAKENED IN THE MEANTIME AND RESUMED HIS WANDERINGS, COULD AGAIN BE HEARD. "WHATEVER YOU DO," HE WAS SAYING, "WHETHER GOOD OR BAD, YOU DO TO YOURSELF."

A Unity that is all-inclusive permits of no "others."

Islands appear to be disconnected pieces of land, but under the sea they are all connected. The seabed, the ground of the sea, connects them all. And so does the Ground of all Being connect us all. "No man is an island, entire of himself," wrote John Donne, "every man is a piece of the continent, a part of the main. . . . "

Whatever you do, you do to yourself.
You are not acting on another, for in reality *there is no other.*[107]

"We created you of a single self" (6:98)[108] means that however diverse and variegated we may be in outward appearance, our innermost core is One. That is why both the Koran (5:32) and the Talmud before it (Sanhedrin, 37a)[109] state that he who saves a human soul saves the world entire, and if he (lawlessly) kills a human being, it is as if he has killed all humanity.

That is why ethical conduct is so important in Sufism—if one wishes to get anywhere, of course. Moreover, God is always responsive but never initially active, because He does not want to interfere with the freedom He has granted human beings. *First* we behave ethically, *then* God responds. First we perform the Formal Prayer, then God participates in it. First we work, then we get paid. "God does not change [what] He has conferred upon a people until they change their own condition" (8:53). Again: "God will never change the condition of a people until they change it themselves (with their own souls)" (13:11).

Whether it is good or bad, large or small, your every action eventually returns to you in a cosmic rebound. I call this "the boomerang effect." "Whoever does an atom's-weight of good shall see its recompense, and whoever does an atom's-weight of evil shall see its recompense" (99:7-8).

Divine justice is closely related to this. It has often been said that the ways of the Lord are mysterious, inscrutable. Yet if we were able to know the whole truth in a particular matter, perhaps we would cease to be perplexed.

THERE WAS ONCE A MAN, RIGHTEOUS AND GOD-FEARING ENOUGH, BUT AT THE SAME TIME UNABLE TO RECONCILE THE PREPOSTEROUS EVENTS OF THIS WORLD WITH GOD'S COMPASSION AND JUSTICE. HE WOULD ENGAGE IN MENTAL QUARRELS WITH GOD. "MY LORD," HE WOULD SAY, "HOW IS IT THAT YOU ALLOW SUCH INIQUITIES, SUCH ABSURDITIES TO OCCUR, WHEN THINGS OF THIS SORT ARE BENEATH YOUR DIVINE PERFECTION?"

ONE DAY, WHEN HE WAS AGAIN ARGUING AWAY LIKE THIS, HE HEARD A VOICE. "ENOUGH IS ENOUGH," THE VOICE SAID. "YOU WILL BE SHOWN HOW DIVINE JUSTICE OPERATES. NOW CROUCH SILENTLY BEHIND THAT BUSH OVER THERE, AND WATCH CAREFULLY."

THE MAN TOOK UP POSITION BEHIND THE BUSH, WHICH WAS NEAR A WATER FOUNTAIN, AND BEGAN TO WAIT. A SHORT WHILE LATER, A HORSE-MAN RODE UP, DISMOUNTED, UNSTRAPPED THE VALUABLE, GEM INLAID SWORD THAT HE WAS WEARING, PUT IT ON THE GROUND, DRANK SOME

WATER, AND WATERED HIS HORSE. THEN HE MOUNTED AND RODE OFF. BUT HE FORGOT TO TAKE HIS SWORD.

BY AND BY, A CHILD ARRIVED TO HAVE A DRINK. HE NOTICED THE SWORD, MARVELED AT ITS GEMS, AND TOOK OFF WITH IT.

SOON AN OLD MAN CAME BY. HE, TOO, WAS THIRSTY. WHILE HE WAS DRINKING, HOWEVER, THE SWORDSMAN ARRIVED IN A FLURRY. HE HAD NOTICED THE ABSENCE OF HIS SWORD AND RETURNED TO CLAIM IT.

WHEN HE COULDN'T FIND IT, HE WAS SUSPICIOUS OF THE OLD MAN. "WHAT HAVE YOU DONE WITH MY SWORD?" HE CRIED. "WHERE DID YOU HIDE IT?" THE OLD MAN PROTESTED HIS INNOCENCE, BUT THE HORSEMAN WAS SO OUTRAGED THAT HE DREW OUT HIS DAGGER AND STABBED THE OLD MAN, WHO FELL TO THE GROUND DEAD. THE HORSEMAN SEARCHED FOR THE SWORD BUT COULDN'T FIND IT. FINALLY, HE RODE OFF.

THE MAN WHO HAD BEEN WATCHING ALL THIS FROM BEHIND THE BUSH COULD CONTAIN HIMSELF NO LONGER. "ALL THIS ONLY VINDICATES WHAT I'VE BEEN SAYING!" HE CRIED, JUMPING UP. "A SERIES OF EVENTS WITHOUT RHYME OR REASON, SENSELESS MURDER—IN OTHER WORDS, THE USUAL STUFF!"

"SHUT UP AND LISTEN!" SAID THE VOICE. "YEARS AGO, THAT HORSEMAN ROBBED THE FAMILY OF THAT BOY YOU SAW. NORMALLY, THE KID WOULD HAVE INHERITED HIS FATHER'S FORTUNE, SO THE HORSEMAN OWED HIM PROPERTY. AND THE OLD MAN YOU SAW KILLED THE HORSEMAN'S FATHER IN HIS YOUNGER DAYS, SO HE OWED HIM A LIFE. DO NOT ASCRIBE INJUSTICE TO THE DIVINE, JUST BECAUSE YOU'RE IGNORANT OF THE FULL FACTS."

Gnosis

Gnosis is the true purpose of man and of existence. As such, it is superior to worship and obeying God's commandments, which are the paths leading to that goal.

For centuries, theologians and philosophers have been debating the existence of God. They have tried to approach the subject by way of rationality. Finally, they have realized that the existence or nonexistence of God is not open to logical proof.

This has led, in our age, to a widespread agnosticism among those who are informed about such debates. Agnosticism holds that it is not possible to know whether God exists, let alone anything else about Him.

But philosophy is not the place where matters about God can be decided. Nor, in reality, is theology, which may be regarded as a branch of philosophy. When you want to decide about the existence of a chair, you do not set about proving it logically. Any prophet, saint, or mystic will tell you that the existence of God is an *empirical* matter, not a logical one. The difference from a chair is that while the existence of a chair is easily determined, God, who is the best-hidden secret of the universe, can be known only by the utmost sustained effort, and then only by a very few. Nevertheless, it is possible. To paraphrase Meister Eckhart, man's predicament is that he wishes to perceive God in the same way he perceives a cow.

The universe is a vast game of hide-and-seek, a cosmic treasure hunt, where the hidden treasure is God. If this is true, we may identify the procedures and practices of Sufism as a map that guides us to the treasure. "Take five steps northward from the gnarled old tree, then turn left and advance ten paces. . . ." One wrong move, and there is scarcely a chance the treasure will be found.

Deep within, human beings have undeveloped organs of perception that can, if cultivated, lead to incrementally increasing knowledge of God. In Sufism, this is known as Gnosis, or "God-knowledge" (*marifat-Allah*).

In contrast to agnosticism, Sufic Gnosis[110] teaches that God can be known. This occurs in three stages. The first stage is theoretical knowledge of God (*ilm al-yaqin*, "the knowledge of certainty," "knowledge without a doubt"). This has been compared to the knowledge of fire that a person who has never seen fire possesses.

The second stage takes us a step further (*ayn al-yaqin,* "the eye of certainty"). As one learns God-science and carries out certain practices, one begins to perceive, if not God Himself, incontrovertible signs of His existence. This has been compared to catching sight of fire from afar.

The third stage is a manifestation that leaves no doubt whatever about God's existence in the mind of the person who has the experience (*haqq al-yaqin,* "the truth of certainty"). At this stage, all doubts are swept away. This has been compared to being burnt and consumed in the fire.

Culmination of Gnosis (*marifah*) is Truth or Reality (*haqiqah*) —in other words, the direct perception of Ultimate Reality, the Ground of all Being.

The most important thing about Ultimate Reality is that He is nondual, i.e., One. Whereas all the realities we know are based on multiplicity, the direct perception of Unity (*al-Ahad*) allows us to conclude that multiplicity is an epiphenomenon and nonessential, if not outright illusory. This process of slowly rising towards the Truth (*al-Haqq*) is also called Unification (*tawhid*).

We should be careful to note that the One we are speaking of here is not a number like any other in the infinite arithmetic sequence: 1, 2, 3. . . . Rather, He is the "One without a second," a Unity so all-encompassing that anything beyond it cannot even be imagined. This may all sound highly abstract and abstruse, but it is a direct and immediate perception in mystical states of consciousness.

The Subject/Object Dichotomy

In nondual states of perception, when the Unity of Absolute Reality (God) is perceived, it becomes clear that there is no subject acting on an unconnected, independent object. For the duality between subject and object is transcended. There is no subject or object (Unity: *ahadiya*). Or, descending one stage lower (Union: *wahidiya*), to the extent that one can talk about subject or object, the object *is* the subject and *vice versa*. Nor can one talk about a multiplicity of subjects or objects from the standpoint of Absolute Unity.

And Absolute, unconditioned, or nondelimited Reality is the Ultimate Ground of all Being from which all relative, conditioned, or delimited realities —"worlds"—emerge.

So even though we live in a world of multiplicity, the truth of that world is actually Unity, although we would be hard put to recognize it as such.

Note that we carefully refrain from equating God with the universe. The universe is *of* God, *from* God, *created* by God (and actively sustained by Him continually). But the universe is *not* God, because God is beyond all worlds and beyond the universe—even though He is also within even the tiniest particle ("the Beyond Within"). To exist in the human condition is our common lot, and from the man's-eye point of view we are not permitted to phrase this in any other way.

If we fail to acknowledge this, we run the risk of collapsing God onto the universe—of saying that the collectivity of all things is God, which is pantheism.

The great Sufi sage Ibn Arabi claimed that the whole of Being is One. For this reason, he has often been accused of pantheism, even though his doctrine of the "unity of existence," of things, of objects (*wahdat al-wujud*), is not intended in that sense. (Ibn Arabi himself never used that term.)

Several centuries after Ibn Arabi, in order to counter this tendency, another great Sufi sage, Ahmed Sirhindi (also called Imam Rabbani, or alternatively "the Renovator of the Second Millennium *anno hegira*"), suggested it would be better to speak of a "unity of observers" (*wahdat al-shuhud*), or souls, or subjects.

Both were right. The two are two sides of the same coin. Of

course, in Ultimate Unity, the object/subject distinction disappears altogether, but until that point is reached, Sirhindi's approach is the more useful and less dangerous one, which also finds support in the sacred verse already mentioned: "We created you (humankind) of a single self." But Ibn Arabi himself never intended pantheism.

Therefore, although we encounter multiplicity in the universe, this multiplicity is nonessential. In actual fact, it is Unity that holds. And for this reason, any action we predicate on isolation, independence, or distinction is falsely conceived. To paraphrase mystical poet Francis Thompson:

All things, by immortal power,
Near and far,
Hiddenly
To each other linked are,
That you cannot stir a flower
Without troubling a star.

This poetic vision[111] has been known to be scientifically true ever since Barry Commoner formulated the first law of ecology: "Everything is related to everything else."[112] Moreover, the concept is receiving physical confirmation as quantum entanglement begins to imply that we live in an infinitely multiply-interconnected universe.[113] (Gravity already weaves together all regions of the cosmos.)

From Gnosis to Ethics

It is possible, then, to go from Gnosis to ethics. We said above that *there is no other,* for we are all parts of a single whole, Totality. Any action originating from any part reverberates throughout the entire structure, expanding outwards like ripples in a pond, is reflected at the nether regions, and converges back on its point of origin. Newton's Third Law, "To every action there is an equal and opposite reaction," is actually a principle of mysticism. And this is the reason why we must "do as we would be done by."

Yet at the same time, there are distinctions to be observed in accommodating that apparent multiplicity. So how do we proceed, how do we tune our actions? According to the Divine Law outlined by Ultimate Reality.

Of course, the Law has diverse ramifications. But here we are interested not in the details, but in the root of the matter. When we view the Law in this way, we see that it is concerned with the rights of all creatures. Even the tiniest ant has its rights when we interact with it, and—this bears emphasis—*man is responsible for rights, and for rights alone.* But what faculty in us recognizes these rights and strongly opposes their violation? It is called conscience.

But conscience itself springs from another faculty, and that is love. I hesitate to call love a feeling, an emotion, because it is more than that—much more. Love is the fabric out of which the entire universe is woven. To quote Idries Shah: "[L]ove exists in different concentrations: or, at least, the feeling of it does. Love, devotion, worship of God, all these are of such sanctity and importance that the Sufis do not use them lightly. . . . [W]hat people fondly imagine as true love has been debased into a mere emotion."[114] And if the Divine Law is based, via conscience, on love, this means that its rules call us to act *as if* we loved the object of our action. For only when we love and respect something can we treat it right; only then can we accord it the same rights we assume for ourselves; only then can we "love our neighbor as ourselves." Even if we do not feel that love, we are protected from Wrong Action by the Divine Law, which prescribes the right behavior—or at least the right attitude—suitable for every relevant occasion.

It is thus that we arrive at ethics.

Sufi Ethics: No Spirituality Without Morality

Sufi ethics can be summed up in four words: no morality, no spirituality. At least, this was how it was exemplified by the Master, and he himself told me that what set him apart from other masters and gurus was his painstaking—or, to my mind, exquisite—attention to morality.

Sufism takes Islamic ethics and practice as its infrastructure, to an extent that those versions of it which do not would have to be called pseudo-Sufism. Probably the first principle of Sufi ethics is the words of the Prophet: "You cannot enter Paradise until you have faith, and you cannot (be said to) have faith until you love one another." The implication is clear: Those who do not love one another cannot enter Heaven. Many stories relate acts of loving kindness and compassion as examples to be emulated. One story that apparently goes back to the Prophet relates how a prostitute was forgiven her sins because she used her shoe to draw water out of a well for a thirsty dog. The Master used to tell us: "If you see a fly in water, save it." Even though the fly is a pest and you may want to swat it when it bothers you, the Right Action when it is in distress is to save it. He also said that even a potentially harmful animal, such as a scorpion, should not be killed unless it is actually harming us.

We cannot know the inner state or station of a God-realized human being. Like everyone else, his inner experience is hidden from our eyes. But we can deduce his quality by his behavior, his ethics, which provide a sure-fire indication. The Godly person is always full of love and compassion towards other beings and acts accordingly, because God's light and compassion flow out of such a person and into the world.

THE FAMOUS PERSIAN SUFI, BAYAZID OF BISTAM (BISTAMI), SAW IN A MOMENT OF UNVEILING THAT THE POLE (SPIRITUAL KING) OF THE AGE

WAS NONE OTHER THAN THE TOWN'S HUMBLE IRONSMITH.

BAYAZID WAS AMAZED, FOR THE IRONSMITH HAPPENED TO BE A MAN WITH FEW DISTINCTIVE QUALITIES. FINALLY, UNABLE TO SUPPRESS HIS CURIOSITY ANY LONGER, HE WENT OVER TO THE SMITH'S SHOP IN ORDER TO TAKE A CLOSER LOOK.

WHEN HE ARRIVED, THE SMITH WAS NONPLUSSED, THREW AWAY HIS HAMMER, AND TRIED TO KISS HIS HAND AS A GESTURE OF RESPECT[115]— FOR BAYAZID WAS OF GREAT RENOWN—AND ASKED FOR HIS PRAYERS.

BAYAZID WAS SURPRISED. HE SAID, "IT IS I WHO SHOULD BE KISSING YOUR HAND AND ASKING FOR YOUR PRAYERS. PLEASE, PRAY FOR ME."

"SURE I WILL," SAID THE SMITH, "BUT I WISH FOR YOUR PRAYERS IN A MATTER THAT HAS BEEN DISTURBING ME FOR A LONG TIME. MY OWN PRAYERS WON'T WORK."

"WHAT'S YOUR PROBLEM?" ASKED BAYAZID.

"I'M WORRIED ABOUT THE STATE OF THE PEOPLE," SAID THE SMITH. "EVERY TIME MY HAMMER DESCENDS ON THE ANVIL AND THE SPARKS FLY, I WONDER HOW THESE HUMAN BEINGS ARE GOING TO WITHSTAND THE FIRE, AND TRY TO FIND A WAY TO IMPROVE THEIR CONDITION."

BAYAZID THOUGHT TO HIMSELF: "SO THIS PERSON IS NOT OF THOSE WHO SAY: 'MY SELF, MY SELF.' RATHER, HE SAYS: 'MY PEOPLE, MY COMMUNITY' [JUST AS THE PROPHET DID]. NOW IT'S CLEAR WHY THE STATION OF POLEHOOD WAS GIVEN TO HIM, FOR HE DESERVES IT.

"MOREOVER, THE POLE OF THE AGE IS SO UNAWARE OF HIS STATION THAT HE KISSES MY HAND AND ASKS FOR MY PRAYERS. SO HE HASN'T RECEIVED UNVEILING YET, AND DOESN'T KNOW WHERE HE IS—THUS DOUBLING HIS SINCERITY."

To be concerned with the troubles of others, to try to ease their pain and heal their wounds, is an act of love and compassion. It is only those who have this in abundance who can rise to the higher stages of Sufi sainthood.

The following Sufic statement, ascribed to Loqman,[116] neatly summarizes Sufi ethics:

In loving kindness, be like the sun;
In generosity, be like water;
In humility, be like the earth;
In hiding the faults of others, be like the night.

To elaborate, the sun rises and sheds its light on all things, without making any distinction between good and bad, worthy or unworthy, etc. Water gives life to both the rose and the thistle without favoritism. The earth continues to lend its bounties to all, taking no heed of who steps on its face. And the night draws a veil of darkness over even the greatest iniquity. The Master used to say that each of these represented a pole, and anyone who was able to emulate even one of them would achieve salvation.

Ethics and Spiritual Transformation

Some of us in the New Age have conceived of inner transformation as an almost mechanical process of energy conversion—as the transformation of one kind of energy into another, or as the subtilization of a coarse form of spiritual energy into a purer or subtler form. Consequently, some people think spiritual transmutation can be realized in a void of morality, without any reference to ethics at all. We cannot conceive that ethical behavior has anything to do with inner metamorphosis. In our technological age, it is perhaps only normal for people to talk about "spiritual technologies."

Now the sublimation of denser energy into finer states does indeed occur. But this cannot be brought about solely by psychic techniques or psychophysical exercises, in a manner analogous to the conversion of electricity into light or heat into mechanical energy. Before such methods can work, one must first put one's accounts with the universe in order, one must settle one's accounts with the cosmos and God. The go-ahead or the signal for "all systems go" must come from every corner, from every one of our interactions with the cosmos and its Creator.

Turkish Sufism has a flavor all its own, and Yunus Emre is one of its most eloquent poets. Here is what he has to say: "Because of the Creator, be tolerant to His creatures." And: "If you have once broken a Heart, the Prayer you perform is void."

The Heart is the throne of God, God looks at the Heart
Whoever breaks a Heart is ruined in both worlds.

What you think for yourself, think also for others
Here, if anywhere, is the meaning of the four books. [117]

This is the foundation, the cornerstone. Look at it this way: you learn the three R's (reading, writing, and 'rithmetic) in elementary school. *But you are never done with them.* All through the rest of your education, you're constantly relying on them at every step, because they're the basis upon which everything else rests. Similarly, you can't pull out the first floor from under a five-story building, just because you have erected the other floors.

The fruit is never a ready-made result waiting for us at the end of the road. It ripens and is infused by our actions, by each and every one of them. Our deeds determine whether the fruit we taste at the end will be full of nectar or poison. This is why ethics provides the infrastructure, and inner transformation is the superstructure built on that.

According to Ibn Arabi, the after-death state, whatever else it might be, is the embodiment of accumulated works and thoughts. Commenting on his philosophy, William Chittick writes: "Not only do people construct their own paradises, they also construct their own hells." As Arabi himself notes: "The chastisement is identical with the actualization of the thought."[118]

There is a delightful Sufi story that graphically brings this alive.

One day, Yunus was allowed to visit Hell in the Imaginal World. He found himself in a vast expanse, a veritable desert. Because he was accustomed to hearing about Hell as a fire and furnace, Yunus was perplexed. How could this place be Hell?

A short while later, a man came by with a great load of wood on his back. He set his load down, arranged it in a pile, set it afire—and stepped into its center.

"What are you doing?" asked Yunus.

"These are my deeds I brought over from the world," the man replied. "Now I must suffer for them."

"But I thought Hell was a huge blazing fire, all ready to consume its inmates."

"No," said the man. "It is only what we bring over, or send over beforehand, that determines what this place shall be for us."

And the same goes for Heaven. Now, to achieve enlightenment means to reach God. In order to reach God, you have to *climb higher than Heaven.* How are you going to reach higher than Heaven, when your actions destine you for Hell?

Let me illustrate with a story. I haven't heard it from anyone, but it is nevertheless a story in the Sufic vein.[119]

The Cane and the Skyscraper

There was a rich mogul who decided to perpetuate his name in stone by building a skyscraper. He gave the job to a construction company, showed them the area where they would build it, and busied himself with his own affairs. After a suitable period, he went to visit the construction site, expecting to find the skyscraper at least halfway done. He was flabbergasted when he saw a gaping hole in place of a tall building. He bellowed so loudly at the construction team at the bottom of the pit that the foreman and the construction engineer came up to investigate.

"What seems to be the problem, sir?" asked the engineer.

"You're going in the wrong direction is what the problem is!" exclaimed the mogul in exasperation. "I'm paying you to build upwards, and here you've gone and dug me a hole instead!"

"Nice cane you've got there, sir," mused the engineer, looking at the cane which the mogul had been waving like a sword. "Have you ever tried to stand it on its tip?"

The mogul stopped. "What's that got to do with it?" he asked suspiciously. "You know that can't be done. I've tried it many times myself," he added. "Here, try it, go on." He passed the cane to the foreman, who took turns with several curious workers in trying to balance it, but to no avail.

"With your permission, sir, may I take a look at it?" said the engineer. He took the mogul's cane and forcefully thrust its tip into the soft soil like a skewer.

The cane stood upright.

"You see," said the engineer, "you can't balance the cane unless a part of it is securely under the ground. And it's the same with a skyscraper. If you want your skyscraper to stand up, you have to make sure part of it is buried. That's what we call the foundation. If you want to raise a hundred-story building, you've got to make sure that the foundation goes down at least seven or eight floors, depending on the texture and stability of the bedrock. That's the reason we're digging this gigantic hole. Before you lay the first stone, you've got to excavate."

The mogul was thus appeased and went off a happier man.

Now just as every building has to have a foundation, so must the Great Work. Liberation or enlightenment is impossible without one. And the foundation for the task of sainthood is—wonderful ethics. It is this which will prevent the sage's skyscraper from toppling at the first wind that comes along. It does not matter how high the mystic's attainment is, because if it falls down it will be of no avail. But if it can remain standing even after a storm, then it is truly unshakable and established permanently.

The Ethics of God

The purpose of creation is man's attainment of God. God created the universe and lowered man into it, in order that man may take the return trip and be raised back up to God. So the more we strive to approach God, the more we are fulfilling our reason for being, not to mention the *raison d'être* of the universe.

But how do we approach God? A saying of the Prophet goes: "Adorn yourselves with the ethics (or: character traits) of God." According to Sufism, God possesses many Names and Attributes. Some of these are essential, some are existential or ontological, and some are . . . ethical. In contemplative Islam, seven attributes have traditionally been counted as the basic attributes of God:

1. Life. God is the Living.
2. Knowledge/science. God is the Omniscient, the All-knowing.
3. Power. God is the Almighty, the All-powerful.
4. Will. God wills anything He desires into (or out of) existence.
5. Speech. God addresses human beings via the signs He has manifested in the universe and communicates with humanity through prophets chosen as recipients of Revelation.
6. Hearing. God is All-hearing.
7. Sight. God is All-seeing.

Now, to "adorn ourselves with the ethics of God" means to shed our animal attributes and clothe ourselves in God's morality, to become qualified by having His ethical attributes. And the more we succeed in doing so, the more closely will we have approached Him. Here are some of the ethical attributes of the Divine that we should invest ourselves with:

1. The more loving we are, the more we approach God as Loving kindness (*al-Wadud*). God's creation of the universe was an act of selfless love, a love so infinite that there is room in creation for both good and bad (God Himself is beyond both). A variant translation of the "hidden treasure" Holy Tradition is: "I was a hidden treasure, and desired to be known. Hence, I created the entire universe through love." God literally *loved* the universe into existence and sustains it through His love even at this very moment. Otherwise, the universe would have no choice but to subside at once into nonexistence.

2. The more honest and truthful we are, the closer shall we approach God the Truth.

3. The more compassionate we are towards our fellow human beings and God's creation, the closer shall we approach God the Compassionate.

4. The more merciful and forgiving we are, the closer shall we come to God the Merciful.

5. Justice is one of the most important attributes of God. The more just we are, the closer we approach God the Just.

6. The more patient and forbearing we are, the closer we get to God the Patient.

And so on. Let me conclude by saying, in short, that God has outlined His requests of human beings in His Book and the Prophet's sayings, and one does not incur God's pleasure by violating them. Obeying those requests allows us to come closer to God by earning His pleasure, and to become more enlightened by God, who is Light (*al-Nur*, 24:35). When this process reaches its climax, that is called Enlightenment, or Realization.

Hence, ethics and inner transformation are directly connected. The latter does not—indeed, *cannot*—occur without the former, since we cannot become Godly or God-realized without fulfilling the labors He has set for us or without partaking in His attributes.

The Role of Faith

Knowledge of God starts with faith in God, with the belief that there is something to be known to begin with: God, who is present with His Being (before the Beginning and after the End), encompassing through His Attributes, known via His Names, manifest in His Actions, and apparent through His works. Faith is the midwife of Gnosis. Unless Knowledge of God is aimed at, nothing much will come from the rote repetition of worship and obedience to God out of habit, although these are in themselves sufficient to secure man's salvation in the afterlife. Faith is only the prelude to experience.

In Islamic Sufism, there is no contradiction between faith and reason because we are not asked to believe in blatant logical impossibilities. The assumptions are few and not irrational. While there is mention of other realities, there is nothing in the rules of logic to exclude the existence of these realities—this is a matter for experience to decide.

Science and Sufism

Observation, hypothesis, and experiment are the guidelines of science. The scientist begins by observing natural phenomena and collecting data about them. Next, on the basis of these data, he frames hypotheses about what they mean, how they are related, and how these observations can lead to further insight. Once the scientist has framed a hypothesis on the basis of observation and logical deduction, the next step is empirical verification. The scientist conceives of and performs an experiment that will settle conclusively whether the hypothesis is right or wrong. He asks the universe a question, and the universe answers. Without hypothesis and experiment, observational data remain just that and nothing more. They do not lead to further knowledge or insight.

So the scientist must do two things: first, he must have enough faith in his hypothesis that he finds it worthwhile to trouble with the experiment. And second, he must *perform the experiment.* But nowadays, experiments are not as simple as rolling a marble off an inclined plane. One has to follow a rigorous, well-designed, intricate procedure step by step using complicated and expensive equipment. Leave out one ingredient from the recipe, and you will end up not with a cake but with a flop.

In Sufism, we are faced with a similar situation. The data we obtain from observing the universe suggest that it is vast and incomprehensible, mysterious and wonderful. What could its secret be, if indeed it has one? We start with the "God hypothesis." Laplace had no need of that hypothesis, of course, but then he was only interested in mechanics. Gnosis informs us that if we perform certain practices, we shall approach God, and finally He will reveal Himself to us. Now the mystics, as Josiah Royce said, "are the most thorough-going empiricists in the history of philosophy," and they are not merely talking through their hats. And as the Islamic branch of mysticism, Sufism too is based on empiricism.

In this respect if no other, then, I find that Sufism shares the methodology of science. Observational data, hypotheses (faith), and experiment (practice) are all there. It is for this reason that I regard Sufism, in part, as a science: *the science of inner states,* a sacred science.

Faith, Love, and Compassion

This is still a very limiting definition of faith, for it is not merely an impersonal assumption that is here at work. Rather, faith is a fundamental component of the human constitution. Human beings have this basic metaphysical yearning to believe in *something,* and even atheists are not exempt from this, although the existence of God is not among their postulates. But the proper object of that yearning is God, for He is our essence from which we have been separated, and we need that essence more than we need oxygen. Nature abhors a vacuum, and if the void in us that belongs to God is not filled by God, then it will be filled by other things. If human beings cannot find wholesome nourishment to satiate their spiritual hunger, then they will settle for surrogates—which, however, provide no real substitute, and may even poison the soul.

Jean-Paul Sartre, despite his atheism, spoke of the "God-shaped hole" in the human soul left by the death of faith. But he found it necessary to reject God whether He existed or not, since the idea of God, he supposed, negates human freedom—which was, of course, Nietzsche's problem also. (Whereas it is quite the opposite, because God is absolute freedom and approaching Him makes us freer.) The crucial question, however, is freedom *for what*, exactly. If the laws of God "enjoin the good and forbid the evil,"[120] are we asking for anything other than freedom for evil when we ask for more freedom? And what possible good is going to derive from unleashing evil? If the freedom of man is not going to serve good, what possible value does it have? Are we asking for the freedom to murder multiples of six million human beings, like a Hitler, or tens of millions of human beings, like a Stalin? Are much smaller concentrations of evil absolved from being evil just because they are less? And are not such unspeakable, unnameable atrocities merely the accumulation of countless lesser evils? When one lives in a coccoon of abstractions, it is quite easy to lose sight of such simple things. And the "God-shaped hole" can only be filled by God again; nothing smaller will do.

All divinely inspired books are based upon love and compassion. The Torah, the Psalms, the Gospel have all preached these concepts. To the extent that a person's actions are not informed by love, the fear of God has restrained people from committing the worst crimes. The Koran, Moslems believe, presents the last, the complete version of God's revelation. It—like its predecessors—teaches peace and love. Those actions that are detrimental to human beings have been called "sins." Even if a believer were driven to extremes, for example, he would not touch what is forbidden (i.e., would not steal). These are the preconditions for our continued survival on Earth. We cannot violate them and still expect to survive—as the case of Nietzsche painfully illustrates.

This chapter begins and ends with Love—as the *raison d'être* of man and as God's mode of acting through the universe. The sacred science of Sufism provides the opportunity for our spiritual transformation and is described as clothing ourselves in "His attributes and ethics." Chapter 3 now provides a more detailed examination of the self from the standpoint of Sufism.

3

SUFI PSYCHOLOGY: AN INTRODUCTION

∽∽∽∽∽

Preliminaries: Body, Spirit, Self/Psyche

The first thing we need is some definitions. The nature of man has traditionally been held to be tripartite. In addition to his outer being, the body (Gk. *soma*), his inner existence has been conceived as having an "I," ego, self, or soul (Skt. *atman* - Gk. *psyche* - Heb. *nefesh* - Ar. *nafs*) and a spirit (Lat. *spiritus* - Gk. *pneuma* - Heb. *ruach* - Ar. *ruh*). The spirit is the difference between a living body and a dead one, i.e., that which animates the body and is considered to survive after bodily death. In other words, the phenomenon of death is nothing but the decoupling or *dégagement* of the spirit from the body. In antiquity, four levels of spirit were contemplated: the mineral, vegetable, animal, and human levels, starting from the simplest and moving towards the most complex. (Yes, even inanimate objects possessed "spirit.")

The self, soul, or I, on the other hand, is the seat of (self-) consciousness; in a loose analogy, the spirit is to the soul as a fruit is to its core or kernel—the two are inseparably connected.

The soul and spirit were considered to be different and distinct entities in both early Hebraism and early Christianity. Yet with the passage of time, the two became confused, so that today the soul, the spirit, and the psyche are considered synonymous, and it is not always clear in usage which of the two aspects one is referring to. This situation derives from the fact that both the spirit and the soul survive after death, as well as from the fact that they both mean "breath" in various languages (see the equivalents given above). As we shall see below, however, the distinction between them is a useful one to maintain. In what follows, therefore, the "self" has been consistently used for the "soul" to avoid confusion, and this terminology is adhered to at least throughout this chapter.

Islamic scholars divided the spirit of man into two parts, as did the ancient Egyptians (*ba* and *ka*) and Chinese (*p'o* and *hun*) before them. The first of these they called the "animal spirit" (*ruh al-haywani*), and the second, the "human spirit" (*ruh al-insani*). What they termed animal spirit was a subtle spiritual substance that comprised the life, sentience, motive force, and will of the body, which man possessed in common with all animals. All the distinguishing higher faculties of man were grouped under the heading of "human spirit."

The following analogy may be useful in conceptualizing the difference between animal and human spirits. Any household item that runs on electricity—a lamp, a washing machine, your TV set—will function when it receives electric power and stop when this is cut off. In this analogy, electricity is similar to the animal spirit ("bioenergy," if you wish). A computer, on the other hand, is a much more complicated device. It, too, needs electricity to run, but it will not fulfill its true function unless you load some software onto it. The software runs on electricity, too, but in a much more sophisticated way: *information is coded into the electronic impulses.* Software, then, is similar to the human spirit in the present analogy. (Please bear in mind that this is an analogy and nothing more—we are not *equating* electric power with the animal spirit or information with the human spirit.) It is the human component of the spirit that survives after death—"information is conserved." The animal component slowly dissipates, subsiding into the immense reservoir of energy (the "infinite bus," in electrical terms) whence it came.

Let us now return to the self. The Sufis and the scholars of Islam called the self associated with the animal spirit—naturally enough—the "animal self" (*nafs al-haywani*), the carnal, egotistical, imperious, or *impelling self*. The self associated with the human spirit, on the other hand, was called the rational or "speaking/reasoning self" (*nafs al-natiqa*), and it is this self which is capable of evolving to the higher stages of selfhood as described in Sufism. But as the animal self is its substratum and the more exclusively human self cannot exist without this, the problem becomes one of taming the animal self and curbing its animal urges. It is only in this way that the more truly human—and divine—aspects of the self can emerge.

A few words concerning "mind" may also be germane at this point. Both *l'Esprit* in French—which Descartes used for *res cogitans*, "the thinking thing"—and *Geist* in German mean simultaneously mind and spirit, so that the two have become confused. But the mind or intellect (Ar. *aql*) is radically different from the spirit (*ruh*). This lamentable confusion in the West, dating from the time of Descartes or earlier but really becoming influential in the nineteenth century, has led to the reduction of spirit to mind and of mind to speech the brain. But that which animates the body and the mental faculties of man are two separate things. More properly, the mind is a faculty—a property and subset—of the human spirit.

Self as Tyrant: The Base Self (Impelling Self)

In the *Arabian Nights*, Sindbad the sailor, during one of his many escapades, is shipwrecked as usual and barely survives, dragging himself onto a strange island where he is washed ashore and falling asleep in exhaustion. When he wakes up, he finds that an ugly pair of legs is entwined around his neck, and that they belong to a drunkard. From that day on, Sindbad becomes the slave of that debaucher, who never relaxes his stranglehold and beats our poor hero on the head until his every whim is satisfied.

Sindbad eventually escapes, of course, but the rest of the story is not our immediate concern. It has been remarked that the *Arabian Nights* contains elements of Sufism, and there is no better example in support of this than the drunkard's deadlock described above, for it is one of the best descriptions in world literature of the essential nature of the base, or evil, self.

Nor, however, is this all. In mythology and fairy tale, in epic and science fiction, we can trace the footprints of the lower self of man: from the seven-headed Hydra (note the number seven!—cf. Chapter 4) to the dragon of St. George, from Mary Shelley's Frankenstein to cyborgs, androids, and killer robots—always, it is the despicable, impulsive, or compulsive self who is the villain, the ogre, the monster. And as mythologist Joseph Campbell aptly pointed out, he who conquers this Minotaur of a self is the hero, *The Hero with a Thousand Faces*. Always it is the same universal story that is retold, under a myriad of appearances and guises. The stories do not usually explain who the villain symbolizes, though this does not detract from their interest or enjoyment; but Campbell has given away the whole show. The enemy is not outside, but within: as the comic character Pogo once remarked, "We have met the enemy, and he is us."

But wait! Where there are dragons, there also are beautiful damsels and buried treasure. Where there is the "dragon of a thousand coils," there also is the Golden Fleece. So what is to be gained by tackling this adversary? Nothing less than something so valuable, so precious, that people of all times and climes have compared it to the hand of a princess or to priceless treasure hoards—not because this was literally true, but because their imagination fell miserably short in attempting to describe what is really involved and could only allude to reality by such metaphors.

It is not simply in past myth or future sci-fi that we encounter the compulsive self, but also in contemporary literature, theater, and cinema—the arts, in short. Picasso's *Minotauromachy* ("Struggle Against the Minotaur") and *Guernica;* Herman Hesse's *Steppenwolf,* part wolf and part man; Oscar Wilde's *Portrait of Dorian Gray,* which becomes uglier as Dorian's misdeeds accumulate; Kafka's portrayal of a man's *Metamorphosis* into an insect, gigantic and revolting; Eugene Ionesco's *Rhinoceros,* which begins as a solitary beast and proliferates like Albert Camus' *Plague* until it encompasses the whole populace, charging to and fro—all are depictions of the domineering self. The writers and artists, the antennae of society, are drawing attention to a psychic malaise which is so widespread that it is now also social—for religion has never been disclaimed to the extent that it has been in the last century.

Now psychology—*psyche-ology,* or "knowledge of the self"—should properly be dealing with this subject. But in modern psychology the pharaonic aspects of the self are confined to the subconscious or id, to which all our meaner impulses are relegated. This is of course important: that the capricious self should have a subconscious component, extending like the roots of a tree underground beyond visibility and frustrating our attempts at conscious control, is certainly a significant discovery. But beyond this, cognizance of the despotic self is scarcely to be found. As for the higher levels of the self and the possibility of evolving to such levels, these lie entirely beyond the imagination of current psychology. Only very rarely in the West does one come across attempts to conceptualize the stages of the self.

One reason for this is that we in the West have been taught that the enemy, the arch-villain, is the flesh, or our instincts, or—

in more recent times—the subconscious. These mistaken diagnoses have veiled the true source of strife from our eyes.

The motto of the carnal self is simplicity itself—from Rabelais' Abbey of Thelema to Aleister Crowley's (of "Golden Dawn" fame), "Do what you will shall be the whole of the law." This, however, overlooks a very simple yet dangerous fact: the more the vagabond self is given free rein, the more it tends to grow. The little squirming worm first becomes a king cobra, then a colossal, fire-breathing dragon—a Tyrannosaurus Rex.

We may be unaware of the presence of the Base Self, but it is there nevertheless. All representations of the Base Self are symbols for a core complex of egotistical drives. And the "damsel in distress" that awaits salvation is the spirit. The choice is between our spirits and our egos; both cannot be free simultaneously. If the inferior self is given free rein, it chokes the spirit. The ego can suppress evidences of the spirit to such an extent that we begin to think we are soulless machines. Hence, in order to elevate and liberate our spirits, we must constrain and confine our egos. Only then is spiritual progress possible, only then can the spirit soar.

The containment of the egotistical self has taken on an added urgency in our day. Thanks to the spin-offs of science and technology, even the humblest person now enjoys privileges undreamt of by the pharaohs and emperors of yesteryear. "Magical boxes" bring voices and images from the other side of the globe; "self-propelled carriages" transport even the poor at speeds no king ever achieved in a lifetime. An African Bushman can communicate with the four corners of the planet. This progressive equalization of previously unheard-of opportunities and goods can only be applauded, and one can hardly think of it as bad.

Yet there is a catch. For the containment of the egotistical self is easy in conditions of scarcity, but difficult in an environment of affluence. Because of the tendency of the inferior self to mushroom in such circumstances, our very luxury may prove our unforeseen undoing.

An ecological perspective is germane here. Not maximal, but sustainable consumption; adherence to the principle of the Golden Mean; taking no more than one's needs even when standing beside a vast ocean—this is how we can keep the commanding self at bay, sustain our standards of living, and contribute to the further democratization of available resources (sharing with others the common wealth of our world) in the midst of plenty.

At the first, entry level, the human or speaking/reasoning self has been subdued by the carnal self and is stuck at this level. The latter commands and impels to evil, for which reason it is termed the commanding or *impelling self*. Its characteristics are bad habits such as ignorance, miserliness, greed, conceit, self-adulation, lust, jealousy, bad manners, and useless activities, as well as making fun of, hurting, and scolding others.

The impelling self is a burden on a human being. It is like an alcoholic son who does every iniquity and leaves his father to mop up behind him.

Now the self, or "I", is a product of God's infinite grace. But being attracted to the world and its intense interest in its own desires has defiled it. It has come under the influence of animal urges, has become bound to lust and thus to animality. It has exchanged its own admirable qualities for the lowly traits of animals, until its only remaining difference from them is outward form. Even Satan gains strength from it. This ugly self is an enemy within us. It is tyrannical and imperious, like a dictator. Furthermore, it emerges from under whatever stone it is lurking at the least expected moment, when we think we have vanquished it, and forces us to fulfill its despicable demands. Only after everything is over do we realize what happened.

This gremlin can only be tamed by self-restraint. Give the

impulsive self its rights, but deny it its pleasures. Abdulqader Geylani, one of the greatest saints, says:

> The rights of the self are the necessary amount of food, drink, clothing, and shelter. Its pleasures are the things it likes, its lusts, and its caprices. Give it its rights in accordance with the measure of the Holy Law. Always feed it with what is Allowed or clean, never that which is Forbidden or tainted. Be content with little, as long as it is allowed. Accustom your self to this.
>
> If you desire liberation, oppose your self where obedience to your Lord is concerned. If your self tends towards obeying Him, concur with it. If it inclines towards error, oppose and struggle against it.
>
> Do not remove the stick of struggle from the back of your self. Do not be fooled by its tricks. It will appear to sleep; do not be taken in. Neither would you be off your guard in the presence of a carnivorous beast that feigns sleep and drowsiness. For it is seeking a chance all the while that it seems lethargic and somnolent. It is in its predatory nature to do so.
>
> Now the self is just like a predator. It acts as if it were sleepy and drowsy, yet the moment it finds its opportunity, it strikes. This self makes a show of external obedience, docility, and compliance with what is good; yet it is hiding the exact opposite within. So be very careful with it in matters where it appears submissive.
>
> Try to heal your self. Say to it: "Whatever good you do is to your own benefit, and what evil you commit is to your suffering. Whatever you do, whether good or ill, will return to you." Struggle against your self. For God has said: "Whoever struggles for Our sake, We shall surely guide to

the straight path" (29:69), and "If you aid God in His religion, He will aid you" (47:7).

Never give the self any room, never tolerate it. Do not obey its demands. Only then will you find salvation and liberation. Never condescend to smile at it. If it tells you a thousand things, answer only one, until you are sure that its behavior is rectified and it is quiescent. If it requests anything belonging to its pleasures and capricious desires, always postpone it, saying: "Wait until Paradise." Accustom it to the patience of want. Never accept a word of what it says. For its propensity is always towards evil. What it wants you to do is evil, without the shadow of a doubt. If you must answer it, let your reply always be negative. Opposition to the self is the road to its edification.

Patience on this path has an end. Patience is temporally finite, yet its fruits are infinite.[121]

Now, I would like to submit that this Sufic concept of the Base Self provides a common denominator, and therefore a bridge, between psychology and sociology. For if it is the operative factor within the ordinary, individual psyche, the same goes for any collectivity composed of such psyches. Hence, this concept yields interesting insights into the social sciences as a whole.

As regards psychology, I would here like to focus on the interpretation of dreams. Various approaches have been developed in psychology for this purpose. The Freudian approach interprets dreams by reference to sex, the Jungian approach in terms of archetypes, etc. The Sufic approach would interpret dream content in terms of the self. This, in my view, is more in tune with the meaning of "psyche-ology." A cat, a dog, a worm, an insect, a toad, a troll, a snake, a monster, a dinosaur, a killer robot, a faceless being would all reflect the Base Self and provide a "pointer reading," as it were, regarding the state it is in at the time of "observation." The process revealed by the dream about this object-symbol would then tell us in which direction the Base Self is moving. As it became purifed, the self would spend more time in positive dream-states—in the company of the elect, for example.

As for sociology, many insights can be gleaned from this Sufic concept. I shall try to outline a few of these below in relation to modernity.

Anthropocentrism

If consumerism is a defining characteristic of our times, a second condition of modernity and post-modernity is anthropocentrism. Man, or more precisely his individual well-being, is taken to be "the measure of all things." This well-being becomes the sole measure of good or bad—which is not entirely wrong in itself, if only we were able to divine its context. But since man does not know what is *really* good for his well-being, mere whims and pleasures become ends in themselves. Humans are not the center of all meaning and the source of all value, and material consumption is not all that being human is about. Otherwise, the highest aspirations of man degenerate into the gratification of individual greed.

One thing is certain: placing man at the center of the universe does not work any more than placing the Earth at the center of the solar system. One reason why it does not work is that we do not take "man" to mean "humanity," but rather "me, myself, and I." When we say, "Man is the measure of all things," we are actually—if only subconsciously—saying, "*I* am the measure of all things."

Thus, we see that a double displacement has occurred. Step One: The Total Self of the universe (namely, God) gets displaced from the focus of attention, and the collective self of humanity is substituted for it. This is a drastic reduction, because no matter how great and wonderful humanity is on the one hand, it is also imperfect, in need of improvement, and insignificant compared to the universe on the other. Totality and perfection are no longer the target, but rather partiality and imperfection. This brings about a stasis. Confucius said, "In order to climb a tree, you have to aim at the stars." In order to achieve true humanity, you have to set your sights beyond man. With perfection no longer the goal, the prospect of psychospiritual progress is vitiated.

What remains is only "horizontal" evolution: progress in the material and technological spheres. No matter how great, this is bound to be one-sided and to belie man's true potentials. The Sufis have compared this to the situation of a king, the ruler of a great kingdom who becomes deranged, goes down to the dungeon, picks up a bone which he thinks to be his scepter, and proceeds to rule the rats, which he mistakes for his subjects.

The devolution of our vision leads on, inevitably, to Step Two: the substitution of man's own self ("I, me") for the self of humanity. Herein lies the rub. Practically unknown outside Islamic Sufism, yet half-suspected in some religious traditions and just below their threshold of consciousness, is the Base Self, which lurks within each of us, has both conscious and unconscious components, and silently plots our destruction. (Freud came close to its destructive aspect when he hypothesized the death instinct or "thanatos.")

So Step Two is really the exaltation—or even the deification—of the Base Self, the ego. Since God has already been derailed in Step One, this Moloch now becomes our new idol. In a Kafkaesque somersault, "Man is the measure of all things" metamorphoses into "My Base Self is the measure of all things." It is true that we do not worship it consciously. Atheists, for example, would deny that they worship anything at all. Yet we worship the Base Self *unconsciously.* Self-love, pride, greed, self-adoration are just the tip of the iceberg that constitutes this worship.

We should take care to distinguish between this demonstrably false meaning of "man is the center of the universe" and its other sense, its true portent. To go "beyond" man is to go to God *through* man. God placed man at the center of the universe, in the middle of past and future eternity and infinite space, at the center of a vast spacetime sphere.[122] We cannot be "anti-man," precisely because God isn't.

The Base Self confronts us with a problem that is difficult to solve. We cannot kill it, for to kill it would mean to kill ourselves. When a person says "I," it is not only his spirit but also his Base Self that is contained in this "I." The only solution is self-purification, by which the Base Self becomes elevated to higher levels of selfhood. And only by aiming at the stars can we climb this tree. We should "strive to become perfect, even as God is perfect." When we have removed all the baseness of the Base Self, then we will have purified ourselves 100 percent, and we shall have attained the Perfected Self. This is the equivalent of the king regaining his kingdom, ascending to his palace, and ruling his land as he did before.

This kind of evolution can only be actualized by psychospiritual progress. It bespeaks a level of human perfection, of maturity and bliss, that we cannot even begin to imagine in our present ground-level (basement) condition. And this is what we have to do if we want to achieve true civilization. For civilization does not mean only material plenty. One can be in a state of material affluence and yet live in Hell. By true civilization I intend not only material but also spiritual well-being, and this can be achieved only by action in its own domain. Ethics is the bedrock on which any spiritual edifice whatsoever is to be founded. If we prove ourselves able to adopt the ethics of the prophets, if we adorn ourselves with the morality of angels, there is no reason why this world should not become a paradise. *And this is the real, though not the whole, point about the prophets and the angels.* They are beacons to man's self-transcendence.

Cyberculture and the Future of Modernity

We may further ask: what of the future? Where, if present trends continue, are we headed?[123] A cultural critic who also happened to be a student of Sufism might make the following observations:

Granting the validity of many other interpretations, it remains a fact that man, with his intelligence and labor, his discoveries and inventions, is the motive force behind technology. If man does not believe in God and does not abide by the rules outlined by God for the benefit of man, he will be ensnared and enslaved by his Base Self. *The Base Self then becomes the engine driving technology, the motor behind civilization.*

Intelligence is of little use here. In fact, the greater the intelligence, the more the Base Self is enabled to do harm. For, supposing a genius to be involved, the Base Self is able to avail itself—somewhat like a computer virus—of all the brain circuits, all the firepower, of that genius. Its capacity to wreak havoc, its ability to cause harm, is correspondingly amplified and enhanced.

At the beginning of the scientific revolution, "Francis Bacon and René Descartes set forth a philosophy of power that founded the modern world view. Guided by the love of mankind, by 'charity' and 'generosity,' they undertook to transform the world into a garden through the conquest of nature, with the aim of eventual planetary mastery by man. . . . "[124] The Base Self relishes power, but since they were in that age imbued with the high morals of Christianity, both men at least tried to harness that power to good ends.

In the sixth and final part of the *Discourse on Method*, Descartes debates with himself whether or not to publicize his discoveries, and is persuaded to do so by the fact that they will be useful to humanity. "In his effort to do great things for others, Descartes gives mankind a method that will lead [in his own words] 'to the invention of an infinity of devices that would enable us to enjoy without pain the fruits of the earth and all the goods one finds in it' . . . "[125] This is, above all, a Christian sentiment, one of altruism and concern for one's fellow man.

Today, however, this inspiration of the Founding Fathers has been lost, along with faith in God, and the Base Self has been released from all its inhibitions. Only to the extent that it survives as an atavism, therefore, will the humanly beneficial use of technology bother hardened hearts and callous consciences. In what Mark Dery calls "Ballard's Rule," sci-fi writer J.G. Ballard identified "the most terrifying casualty" of the twentieth century as the "demise of feeling and emotion." Idolaters are cursed by progressively becoming like their idols—they turn into what they adore—and mechanolaters or cyberlaters have similarly been doomed to become increasingly unfeeling and insensitive. Everyone else, watch out! All those evil cyborgs and killer robots you see in movies are images of the Base Self—in a technological setting—bubbling up from the psyche.

Man has always fashioned his idols with his own hands and then worshipped them. Where a satisfactory faith in God is absent, the adulation of the machine and the deification of technology, a Sufi student would say, are the natural outcomes of an unrestrained Base Self and an unguided—or rather, misguided—spirit. Technology confers on man both power and a sense of power. And power (plus sex) is what the Base Self is mainly interested in. We have already seen in Chapter 1 that power seduces the Base Self beyond its wildest dreams, which in turn gives thanks to the machines that have placed so much in its hands by worshipping them.

If man is imperfect and machines superior, the more closely man ought to approach perfection the more mechanized he gets. The notion of a cybernetic organism, or "cyborg," has been in the air for a long time. Ultimately, one's mental patterns would be transferred to a machine, getting rid of the human body altogether. This prospect, however, is viewed with euphoria by some and with anxiety by others, for the perfection of the man-machine symbiosis also spells the demolition of man.

This is a mere continuation, when viewed in perspective, of religious loathing of the flesh and the fear of death. Since we now believe that we do not possess immortal souls, but rather are supposed to be composed of bioelectronic currents in the brain, immortality is to be attained by "downloading" those currents into a suitable machine. This is supposed to be an improvement over the human condition, based on a body that is full of fluids, messy, and prone to sickness and pain, old age and death. The idea has been around for a long time in science fiction. In one dominant theme, extraterrestrials superior to us are supposed to transfer the patterns of information that are "their selves" into robot bodies, and then to evolve, over a vast timescale, into beings of pure energy.

The student of Sufism, however, would maintain that what these hypothetical aliens evolved to in thousands or millions of years, *every human being now possesses as a natural birthright by virtue of one's immortal soul,* and that we have not yet fathomed *the perfection of a fully awakened body harnessed to a fully enlightened spirit,* infinitely beyond the possibilities of any machine, however wondrous.

There is, therefore, another possibility beyond what is offered us by our present civilization. It paradoxically unites both alternatives viewed as mutually exclusive or contradictory in that civilization: the harmonious togetherness and development of the body and the spirit. We can either remain within the confines of such contradictions or move on to an exhilarating synthesis—that provided by the Sufi vision of things.

The radiant future, the immense potential promised us by the cyberprophets, *we possess already.* All we need to do is become aware of it, open up to it here and now, using the techniques of Sufism. Machines and computers are "all right" in themselves; it is only when they are made into a be-all and end-all that the healthy balance is lost. Man impoverishes himself by expecting too much from machines and too little from himself. But man is always superior, since the computer emerged from man and not the other way around. In producing Artificial Intelligence, what man effectively does is take his own intelligence and place it in the machine. The machine does not create its own intelligence independently of man. If we can keep matters in proper perspective, machines can continue their role of helping man and not harming him. Otherwise, man will be enslaved by his own slaves.

Higher Stages of Human Existence

The enemy is the Base Self. Not the *body,* but the *Base Self.* This distinction is so important that it cannot be overemphasized and bears repeating a hundred times. For two thousand years, this has been our main failure in the West: we identify the body with the opposite of good. Even among our highest mystics, or in those opposed to Christianity, this belief has held sway.

This assumption has caused no end of trouble down the centuries. Inhuman psychophysical techniques, ostensibly for the improvement of man, have overtaxed people, mangling and mutilating them. The result is abnormal, unnatural, inhuman, and mentally unhealthy, ending frequently in psychopathology: stupor, sadomasochism, and other forms of imbalance. Another outcome is that these methods turn their practitioners into impersonal robots—into cogs or wheels of an institutional machine.

We should never confuse the root problem. *It's the self. It's not the body.* "Sound body, sound mind" should be our motto. Mortification of the body must never be attempted without proper supervision, and in any case there is no longer any need for this. The sultan Ibrahim Adham, like the Buddha, had to abdicate his throne and riches in order to become a dervish. Later on, when his trials were related to Abdulqader Geylani, the Grand Sheikh remarked: "If he had lived in our time, we would have enabled him to achieve realization without leaving his crown and his throne."

In short, Sufism tells us that the assumption is mistaken. It is not the body that is bad. Nor must we transform body into spirit and become walking ghosts. Rather, it is a fine-tuning of the harmony between the body and the spirit that is called for, a transformation of the mind-body complex—or, since the mind is a subset (or subfunction) of the human spirit, the spirit-body complex. And the main obstacle in this goal is . . . the Base Self.

But the Base Self is not the only option available to man. On the contrary, it is merely the starting point, the basement level. Beyond it, the Sufis have outlined the *accusing, inspired, serene, pleased, pleasing,* and *perfect* (or perfected) levels of selfhood. The concept of the Base Self affords us multiple insights into the human condition. But it is far more interesting and exciting for us to explore what we have the potential to *become.*

The Sufis have developed two major approaches to psycho-spiritual evolution. The first of these is *the path of the self,* where the main emphasis is on self-purification. The second is *the way of the spirit,* which involves work on the subtle body and psychic centers. The second, however, cannot totally neglect the first. Hence, we shall continue our discussion with a treatment of the self-based approach, and then turn to the spiritual path. These are discussed in the context of a Sufi order, or spiritual school, where a teacher/student or master/disciple relationship holds.

Such schoolwork does not imply asceticism or the life of a recluse. The Master achieved everything from within a normal, married, workaday life.

●━●

In this chapter we have described in detail the nature of the Base Self and its gravitational pull away from The Light, showing the consequences of a culture driven solely by a deified ego. It was stressed that man's enemy is not the body but the compulsive self. Chapter 4 now presents "the path of the self" as a method of achieving human perfection.

4

THE WAY OF THE SELF

The real devil is the self of man.
—FAKHRUDDIN RAZI[126]

Stage 1. The Base Self

We have already seen in detail what the Base Self means. To recap, this is the ground level of human psychic development, and it always dictates evil. The concept of the egotistical or Base Self (*nafs al-ammara*) is firmly rooted in the Book (12:53). This dastardly self colludes with the external principle of evil and is responsible for most of human misery. Because human beings are originally born good, however, they have the ability to purify themselves and to rise above this stage. In this chapter, we shall summarize the dangers that await the seeker on the path. [127]

In the initial stages of the journey of the self, the seeker is in danger of falling easy prey to illusions and vain imaginings. The "spirit of gravity," the regressive principle that tries to pull us down, is always striving to thwart a human being from soaring, from spiritual evolution and elevation. When the traveller is at the stage of the impelling self, he is bombarded with the following suggestions:

"What business have you with this path? All those who have entered it are dead. Only their words and their books remain. I know you want to enter the Path of Truth. But who is there to guide you? Show me, where are the people of lofty attainment, of great Struggle and Observation, who are able to work miracles? That was in the past. Nowadays, you cannot even find one of their kind. The best thing for you is to remain with the Holy Law, be content with it, and seek help from the dead saints."

But this is a deception. Perfect human beings, mature masters and teachers, exist in every age. If the traveller heeds these untruthful suggestions, he will reduce his efforts and struggle in the path of the Spiritual School, his enthusiasm will cool, and a timidity in continuing the journey will overcome him. In that case he becomes vulnerable to the next step of the deception:

"God is forgiving. He loves those who act with License towards permitted things. Stop treating your self cruelly. Treat it with tenderness, so that it may obey you."

License (*ruhsah*) is the opposite of Restraint (*azimah*), which is defined as exercising control in performing things that are Allowed (*halal*)—in other words, erring on the side of caution. If the traveller indulges in license, his notion of what is permitted and what is Forbidden (*haram*) begins to get confused, and as a result he approaches the border of prohibitions. As his doubts increase, darkness invades his heart, and he finally winds up yielding to prohibitions.

(Basically, good deeds arising from charity, kindness, etc., are considered Allowed and are associated with light and cleanliness. Bad deeds such as stealing and embezzling are Forbidden and are associated with darkness and pollution. Both are contagious. For example, if you visit someone who has stolen something and eat food bought with that stolen money, you too become contaminated with that darkness.)

If, however, God comes to the rescue, the traveller will be able to identify all these as delusions and say: "To pursue License is for the lazy. To act according to it is for weaklings. It is necessary to follow the manners dictated by Divine Law and the principles of the School." If the traveller can do this, his self will rise to the second stage, the stage of the Critical Self. From the prison of the carnal self, it takes wing to the space of divine spirit. If he is able to persevere to the end, his pride is transformed into humility, his hatred into love, his callousness into tenderness, and his lust into chastity.

Stage 2. The Critical Self

The second station of the rational self has been called "critical," "reproachful," or "soul-searching" (*lawwama*, 75:2) because it repents of commanding evil and blames itself. Some traits of the compelling self still survive in this stage, but there exists the ability to discriminate between truth and falsehood, good and bad. The Critical Self is disturbed by the disgusting traits it finds within itself but is incapable of completely shedding them. It loves the Divine Law and the spiritual schools, however, and it has many good deeds to its credit, such as Prayer, fasting, and charity. Still, covert hypocrisy remains mixed in with them.

The possessor of this self wants his good works to be known by the people. He does them both for God's sake and for show. He is revolted by this habit, however, and cannot find solace. But he is also unable to get rid of it.

Those in this station have, of their own choice, decided to die to their selves and to exist with God and have entered the path of dying by their own volition before physical death overtakes them. The Prophet said, "Die before you die," and Moses said the same thing to his people: "Slay your selves" (2:54). What is meant by "self" here is the ego—namely egotism, self-aggrandizement, and egocentrism. Suicide is definitely not implied.

It is necessary to continue on one's way without tarrying in this station. For there is great danger and an eroding weariness at Stage 2. Those who remain there cannot find comfort or salvation.

The two dangers of this stage are arrogance and anger. Of these, anger is said to be composed of the same fire that Satan was made of. Indeed, when his wife Aisha was angry, the Prophet said: "This is the fire which has been called 'the place of Satan'."

This state of fury is an extremely dangerous and accursed enemy for its owner. And the root of this bad habit is arrogance. To eradicate conceit from one's self is the best of all cures.

Anger and conceit have three antidotes:

1. When conceit is gone, it will be found that anger has vanished of itself. As long as the cause of conceit remains, anger cannot be expelled. The cause of conceit is a full stomach. This strengthens conceit to the extent that anger borders on depravity. Hunger and sleeplessness should therefore be cultivated, and conceit should be uprooted with hunger.

2. The best antidote for the stimulus of anger is to think of one's self as weak, and thus to consider oneself unjustified in attacking another. One must threaten one's self with the bitter fruits of anger and the retribution of God. Kindness, affection, and gentleness are necessary, but overcoming anger is even more necessary.

3. Another antidote for anger is this: If you are standing when you get angry, sit down; if you are sitting, stand up. If possible, take an Ablution, lie down face upwards, and recite the following prayer: "My Lord, enrich me in knowledge, decorate me with

gentleness, grant me worship and fear of You, bestow well-being and health upon me. Amen."

All beings envy the wayfarer and try to prevent him from experiencing the presence of God. In return, that person should not favor anything or be afraid of anyone.

Delusions make one's actions appear lovable to a person in this station and thus introduce feelings of self-love into his heart. The line of thinking is somewhat as follows:

"You have now learned everything. From now on, you have no need to gain further knowledge, or to join the discussion groups of the wise and knowledgeable, or to listen to the sermons of preachers. If only that man of knowledge or preacher would advise his own self and perform even a tenth of your deeds!"

As a result of this deceit, the person becomes so conceited that he does not heed a single word of advice from his guide. He does his worship according to his own mind and is wasted away in the darkness of ignorance.

As can be seen, the tricks and deceptions that prey on the seeker are legion. The propensity to delude oneself will wreck the deeds of the traveller if it can; and if it cannot, it will then instill the wish of a better deed in the seeker's heart—so superior to his works and capacity that he will be incapable of performing it. This deed will appear much worthier to the disciple, and he will be forced to attempt it, but in his struggle to achieve this higher goal, the wayfarer forsakes even his lesser accomplishments. Thus, he loses both.

For example, one such red herring may be excessive charity, in spite of the fact that the seeker is not rich. The disciple gives all he has and becomes destitute. His heart begins to darken, he postpones his Prayers, he starts to gossip, swear, and engage in other bad deeds. Whereas he was earlier a lighthearted, good-natured fellow, comporting himself with gentleness and regarding others as superior to himself, he now begins to criticize people and regard them as inferior because of his travails. He becomes ill-mannered, his heart becomes troubled; his self miserly, covetous, and critical of others. The ruse of the delusion has succeeded.

If God's grace and salvation reach out to this disciple and protect him from such delusions, that person can be raised to the third station by diligently practicing the etiquette of the Sacred Law and the requirements of the mystical schools.

Stage 3. The Inspired Self

The self in the third station is called *inspired* (*mulhimma*, after 91:7-8) because it receives flashes of inspiration from the Divine without any intermediary. Although superior to the reproachful self, this too is a dangerous station and needs the guidance of an enlightened master to handle it. Otherwise, it is quite likely that a relapse to the previous stage will occur.

The fact is that this station, while superior to the preceding two, is still not secure against the seductions of the "spirit of gravity" or the ego. Because it also receives inspirations from God, it confuses the one with the other.

At this stage, the tendency to delude oneself aims at dissolving the ties between the student and his master. Under the guise of a divine inspiration, the master is made to appear in a bad light in the seeker's eyes. This may appear quite authentic, and the only way to detect its falsehood is by the content. But since the master is actually a mirror to people, the ugly characteristics that the disciple projects upon him are none other than his own. The lifesaver that the student must cling to on these stormy seas is the Divine Law. In particular, the Prayer must be performed with great attention to its details. If this gives rise to arrogance and feelings of superiority in him, he cannot rise to the rank of those close to God and remains only in the rank of the good. But if he intentionally discontinues Prayer, he will be reproved and deprived of the spiritual pleasures of Prayer. A condition of love is that the lover obey every wish of his Beloved.

In this station, the traveller is prone to experiencing "loss-of-self." While in this state, the disciple forgets everything he knows, sees wrongly, understands wrongly, and is mistaken in general. The sense organs convey erroneous impressions and perceptions to him. However, this state has nothing to do with the "extinction in God" experienced at a later stage, and should not be confused with it.

Delusions are still in hot pursuit of the traveller in the third station. Appearing to side with truth, they whisper: "You have now seen, heard, and understood everything. You have become a sage. Why should you need to perform all these arduous deeds any longer? From now on, what becomes you is this: Leave all the worship and work that belong to outer appearance to the externalists. Try to invest your time with internal worship, with concentration and contemplation. Contemplate God and try to see Him. These are more important and necessary than external worship."

If the disciple is taken in by these suggestions and abandons worship and struggle, his heart begins to darken, and deceit gains a foothold there. Once this is achieved, the next suggestion is:

"You are the truth of your Lord, and He is your truth. You have now become a saint. All the observances and limitations incumbent upon mortal servants have been lifted from you. Therefore, you can do whatever you please or desire. Everything is permitted for you. You will not be held accountable."

This is one of the most insidious deceits imaginable, for everything can be permitted only if one denies God. As the Great Sage

Geylani once said, "The Lord never wants His Prohibitions to be transgressed and will never order anyone to do so."

When this happens, the veils of darkness engulf the physical and spiritual sight of the disciple to such a degree that he becomes completely incapable of seeing the truth. He does not hesitate to commit any iniquity, such as theft, treason, fornication, or drinking. His faith is corrupted entirely. He ceases to fear God. He becomes such a plaything of deceptions that he leaves Truth aside and makes untruth his leader. Such is the sorry end of anyone who heeds delusion.

If God's grace rescues this person, if he remains firm in worship and struggles with love and diligence, his self rises to the fourth station.

Stage 4. The Serene Self

The human or rational (speaking/reasoning) self in the fourth station is content, its heart is assured, and its sorrow dispelled by the speech of its Lord. This is why it is called contented, tranquil, or *serene* (*mutmainna*). It is the product of sustained effort in a spiritual school. The self at this level has attained a pretty good idea of where it comes from and where it is going.

The disciple does not show the slightest deviation from the Holy Law in this station. He takes pleasure in practicing the moral conduct of the Prophet, and his heart is contented by following the Prophet's example in actions and behavior. Everything he says is in harmony with the Book and the Traditions. Therefore, those who listen to him never tire of listening, for the truths and subtleties poured into his heart by the Lord come alive in his words. He enlightens those around him, occupying himself with worship and invocation most of the time. He has won most of the approved qualities and become invested with generosity, trust in God, surrender, patience, hope, righteousness, kind-heartedness, cheerfulness, thanksgiving, hiding others' shames, forgiveness, and joy of heart. He does not care for the paranormal feats that may manifest from him, binding himself to God, who is the true source of such phenomena. He knows that being partial towards these is shameful and leads one astray. Perfect men do not know the psychic achievements exuding from them, and if they do, they don't attach importance to them; in fact, they try to hide them.

For the perfect person truly in love with God, all thoughts that do not accord with the Sacred Law are in error. *Every external decree of the Holy Law has a secret—an internal—counterpart.* But he who does not abide by its clear, outer precepts can become neither a saint nor perfect. The treasures of the Divine Law remain hidden to him. He may even lose faith and become perverse.

But the person who has attained the fourth stage has, after great struggle and hardship, finally been able to overcome the Base Self. He abides by God's Commandments and the Prophet's Way in every move and deed. These two are the only lifesavers and branches to hold on to in tempestuous seas. Hence the traveller reaching this station has definitely curbed the Base Self, and while it always exerts an influence, it is now tamed and easier to contain. From now on, progress to subsequent stages takes place in quick and easy steps. This is indicated in the verses: "*Contented Self,* return to your Lord, you being *Pleased* with Him and *Pleasing* to Him" (89:27-28).

Stage 5. The Pleased Self

The human self in the fifth station is called the *pleased* (*raziya*) self because it has achieved mature joy in all respects: it remains pleased with God no matter what befalls it. The initial signs of Unity begin to manifest themselves.

The self in this stage experiences peacefulness and surrender, avoids Prohibitions, loves with a pure heart, abandons everything, and forgets everything except God. The person accepts every event in the world with calmness and placidity, without objections. Because he is in control of his self, he does not approach forbidden or objectionable things. God always accepts his prayers. But his excessive shame and humility prevent him from praying; he is ashamed to request anything of God. He prays only in an emergency, and his prayers are sure to be accepted. He is honored in the sight of the Lord. He is seated on such a throne in the inner world that the whole outer world awaits his command.

Stage 6. The Pleasing Self

The rational self in the sixth stage is called the *pleasing* (*marziya*) self because it is pleasing to God. Many of the signs of Unity now become manifest. This is the penultimate stage of human psychological evolution. Unity is not yet permanently established.

The person at this level is clothed with the morality of God. He has departed from human desires and become fair-mannered. He forgives sins, hides shames, and always thinks well of others. He is kind, generous, and altruistic towards everyone. He loves and tends towards people, trying to rescue them from the prison of nature—and the darkness of the ego—into the light of the spirit. This love is only for the sake of God, which is why it is so valuable. The pleasing self combines the love of creatures with the love of God.

The one who is at this station is moderate in everything he does. He neither exceeds nor falls short. This temperate attitude is apparently easy, but very difficult to achieve in reality. Everyone wants to possess this wonderful asset. But few ever do, because it is an extremely difficult state to maintain. It is a grace and boon belonging to those in this station alone.

To the mature person at the sixth stage, the first good signs of the great viceregency begin to appear. At the end of this process he is dressed in all the regalia of that rank. The servant knows all the subtle secrets of things through the knowledge given him by His Lord. God has informed His servants of these secrets with the proclamation: "I taught Adam the names of all things." There are secrets associated with this stage that cannot be expressed in words. It is impossible for anyone not possessing this state to comprehend these, for they do not have correlates in the external world to which they might be compared.

Stage 7. The Perfect, Pure, or Complete Self

The human self that has risen to the seventh station is called the *perfect self* because it has reached the pinnacle of maturity, and the purified or *pure self* (*safiya* or *zakiya,* after 18:74, 87:14, 91:9) because it has become completely purified. The seeker can rise to the sixth stage by struggle, but the seventh can only be bestowed on him by the grace of God. This is the final stage of human evolution, where all human potentials manifest themselves in full bloom. It is also the level at which the mystery of Unity is fully revealed. The consciousness and knowledge that obtain at this stage have been called "objective consciousness" and "objective knowledge" because there is no trace left of the delusions generated by the Base Self.

The seventh station is the highest and most exalted station of all. The Inner Kingdom (the Kingdom which, as Jesus said, "is within you") has reached perfection, and the struggle is finished.

Asceticism and self-restraint are no longer necessary. It is enough to avoid excess in all things. The possessor of this stage has no desires left, for they have all been granted. He still continues, however, to wish for the pleasure of his Lord.

The actions of the perfect human being at this stage are all goodness and worship. His sweet breath is power and grace. His gentle speech is knowledge and wisdom, sweetness and light. His blessed face radiates peace and joy. His sweet and effective speech is soothing, peaceful, and affectionate.

The person at this stage is never without worship, even for a moment. He worships with all his bodily organs, with his tongue, hands, and feet, or solely with his heart, and is never heedless of his Lord.

Such a person repents frequently. He is extremely humble. The tendency of people to seek God pleases him greatly. He is sad and offended if they neglect God. He loves those who desire and love God more than he would love his own child. Both his love and his anger are not for his self, but for God alone. Everything he does is right. He acts with justice in everything. His every wish is in accord with God's wishes. As we shall see in the last chapter, he is one who has attained "the Station of No Station."

◗━◗

This chapter has detailed the transition of the self through stages of perfection: from the Impelling through the Critical, the Inspired, the Serene, the Pleased, and the Pleasing, until Final Purification is reached. Chapter 5 now examines "the path of the spirit" and the spiritual body.

5

THE WAY OF THE SPIRIT

The Subtle Body and Its Anatomy

In the last chapter, we covered one of the two paths of Sufic development: the path of the self. It is now time to look at the second path. And in order to do so, we need to consider the spiritual body, or "energy body."

Recognized in many traditions, the "subtle body" is a non-material form of body that connects the physical body and the spirit. To Henry Corbin we owe the appealing coinage "Imaginal World"[128] with reference to the Sufic term *alam al-mithal,* which describes an interworld or intermediate world between matter and spirit/mind. This is the world of spiritualized substance or substantiated spirit. It is the abode of thought-forms or idea-images, for each abstract thought makes its appearance in this world in a concrete symbolic form. Milk, for instance, stands for knowledge, and drinking milk is the symbol for increasing one's knowledge. Because it stands midway between Descartes' *res cogitans* and *res extensa*—because it is a world where ideas have extension and form—it bridges the mind/matter dichotomy and saves us from the paradoxical aspects of the duality of the material world versus the intelligible world.

Now the subtle body is itself a part of this Imaginal World (which is definitely not imaginary). It is a congealment from the World of Spirits (*alam al-arwah*), and couples the spirit with the physical body. It normally has the form of the physical body that it is coupled to, but this form can change depending on the inner reality of the person in question.

Because it possesses form and extension, it makes sense to talk about a *subtle physiology* or *psychic anatomy* in connection with the subtle body. It is due to this fact that we are able to speak of "Subtleties," or subtle centers (pl. *lataif,* sing. *latifa*) belonging to this spirit-body.

We have already seen that man possesses a spirit. This spirit is coupled to the physical body in the form of a *spiritual body.* Now this subtle body possesses a *psychic anatomy* or structure, just as the material body has a physical anatomy. When Sufis speak of the Heart, for example, what they have in mind is not the physical lump of flesh that pumps blood throughout the body. Rather, they refer to the heart of the spiritual body, which animates the physical body as long as a human being is alive.

In the same way, there are other psychic centers within the spiritual body akin to the Heart center, and it is to these that the term "Subtleties" applies.[129]

These psychic centers are variously referred to as the Five Subtleties (Figure 1), the Seven Subtleties, or the Ten Subtleties. All ten Subtleties are shown in Figure 2.

The five basic subtleties are located in the chest (*Sadr*). These are the Heart (*Qalb*), the Spirit (*Ruh*), the Secret (*Sirr*), the Hidden (*Khafi*), and the Most Hidden (*Akhfa* or *Ikhfa*).

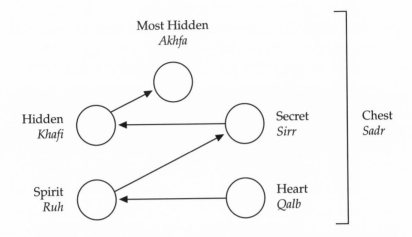

Figure 1. The Five Subtleties *(lataif)*.

In order to obtain the seven subtleties, the Self (*Nafs*) is added to the beginning of this list, and the Human Self (*Nafs al-natiqa*, or Speaking/reasoning Self) is added to the end. Sometimes the Self (*Nafs*) is omitted, and the Total (*Kull*) is added to give the seven subtleties.

An intermediate stage called the Secret of the Secret (*Sirr al-Sirr,* or S^2), and two further centers beyond the Human Self—the Throne (*Kursi*) and the Highest Heaven or Empyrean (*Arsh*)—complete the list of ten subtleties. Occasionally a further center, the Total (*Kull*) or the Universal Intellect (*Aql al-Kull*), is inserted between the Human Self and the Throne. (This may be considered a subcenter of the Throne.)

Further information concerning these subtleties is outlined below. (All measured distances are approximate. The colors and locations of the centers are sometimes listed differently.)

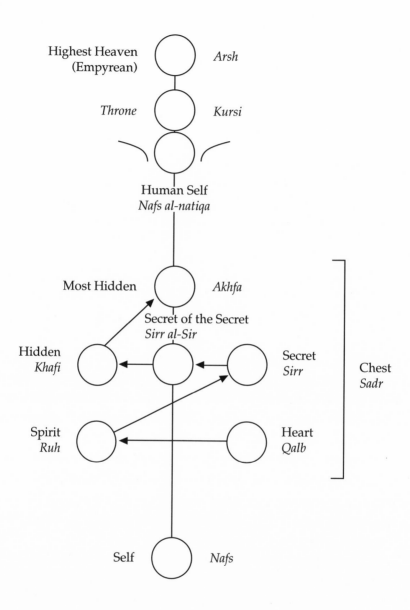

Figure 2. The Ten Subtleties *(lataif)*.

The Self: This is the center of the animal (animating) self, corresponding to the *Hara,* or Life Center, of the Japanese. It is located within the body an inch below the navel or belly button.

The Heart: Also called *Fouad,* this does not actually coincide with the physical heart (which is more centrally placed) but is located an inch below the left nipple. It is associated with the color red and the prophet Adam, "whom God purified."

The Spirit: Its location is an inch below the right nipple. Color: yellow. Prophet: Noah, "whom God saved."

The Secret: Location: an inch above the left nipple. Color: white. Prophet: Moses, "who talked with God."

S^2: Location: center of the chest (between Secret and Hidden). Color: black. Prophet: Jesus, "the Mystery of God."

The Hidden: Location: an inch above the right nipple. Color: green. Prophet: Mohammed, "the Beloved of God."

The Most Hidden: Location: top of sternum (just below the neckline). Colorless. In some charts this is called the Axis of the Secret (*Mustawa al-Sirr*).

The Human Self: Location: between the two eyebrows. According to some Sufis, this is the station of *Qaaba Qawsayn,* "the distance—or meeting—of two bows/arcs" (eyebrows) (53:9). Color: ochre.

The Total and/or *the Throne*: Location: center of the forehead. This is where, at a certain stage of development, the famous "third eye" opens. (Please note, however, that the third eye has nothing to do with physical anatomy, such as the pineal gland, as Descartes claimed.)

The Highest Heaven (Empyrean): Located at the crown or topmost point of the head. Corresponds to the *Sahasrara Chakra* (the "thousand-petaled lotus") in Yoga. (These correlations with other traditions are mentioned not because the Sufic conception was taken from these as sources, but in order to highlight the fact that corresponding realities have also been recognized in other traditions, since truth is one.) This is where divine light—called "the most sacred effusion" (*fayz al-aqdas*) by the Sufis—appears, initially in the form of a star. This location also corresponds to the juncture of the cranial bones, and in some traditions it has been considered the entry point of the soul into the body (the bones are not joined in the newborn baby, but close in later on).

Now that we have formed some idea about the subtleties, how does one utilize this "tree of life"? Basically, the procedure is to activate the psychic centers in ascending order. One starts by concentrating on the chest area (*sadr*) as a whole. (Note that its color, blue, is also the color of a healthy psychic aura.) One then concentrates on the Heart subtlety, and so on in accordance with the direction of arrows in Figure 1. Each center is awakened by concentrating the invocation appropriate to that stage in that center. For instance, *Allah* is the invocation proper to the Heart center. Once an invocation becomes fixed or permanent in its center, and light of a color specific to that center becomes manifest (as well as certain other signs), the center is considered to be "conquered" or "opened." One then passes on to concentrating invocation in the next center.

Warning: Note that one must not try to awaken any center without the permission of a qualified master. This is very dangerous. Do not try to "teach yourself," and don't experiment. Without proper guidance, you're liable to get lost in God-knows-what sector of inner space.

God has stated in a Sacred Tradition: "Know that there is a [physical] heart in each body. There is a *Fouad* [spiritual Heart] in each heart. There is a Secret in each spiritual Heart. There is a Hidden in each Secret, and there is a Most Hidden in each Hidden. I am in that Most Hidden."

This "withinness" should not be compared or confused with physical contiguity. It has no quality and quantity, and it is different from whatever may occur to the mind.

Cornering the Ornery Self

The way of the spirit is interesting, but the seeker's progress cannot be consolidated if one falls victim to the Base Self. Without mastering that, there is always the danger of returning to square one, if not worse. All the painstaking work invested in opening the psychic organs can be wasted before you know it. This is why the way of the spirit cannot be pursued independently, but must always advance in conjunction with the way of the self.

The Master never tired of emphasizing how important self-mastery is. In his view, mastering the Base Self was the key to enlightenment, and indeed the prerequisite of all spiritual progress. "The greatest thing," he said, "is to control the self. The second greatest thing is to have compassion for all creatures. The third greatest thing is to fulfill Islamic principles to the letter.

"We warn a child who approaches a stove: 'Don't touch it, you'll get burnt,' yet he touches it all the same, and although he gets hurt, later on he wants to touch it again. We are just like that.

"The Base Self tells us: 'Do this, do that. I like, I do not like.' The great saints have all controlled their selves. Whatever the self told them, they did the opposite, they curbed it. The Base Self continues its influence even in the greatest of them.

"I treat my self as if it were a child. I say 'no' to everything it wants, only I give it a little of what it wants [provided it is Permitted] in order to shut it up. In this way I silence its proddings, such as 'You're hungry, you haven't eaten,' which would otherwise never end.

"It is impossible to do anything before the self calms down, before it subsides. A seeker once went to a teacher: 'Put me in shape,' he said. But because the self ceaselessly vibrated, shook, and attacked right and left, nothing could be accomplished. The teacher can stop this trembling, but it is the duty and responsibility of the seeker to do this. The same seeker went back to the teacher after he had brought his self to a quiescent state, and this time he saw that everything proceeded smoothly. Nothing can be done unless the self settles down, because the rebellious self will also prevent Islamic principles from being practiced. The tiniest opportunity is enough for the self to ruin everything.

"In trussing up his self, in reining in and restraining its every dash and impulse, the seeker should think that it is actually his teacher who is doing this from within him. He should not attribute it to himself. [Otherwise, this too becomes fodder for ego-inflation.]

"What is required from you is not service. More than that, it is for you to restrain your self. Without bringing the self to quiescence, the seeker cannot clothe himself in his teacher's ethics, cannot achieve his teacher's state, and cannot moralize himself with his morals."

If I may be allowed to interpret this by drawing a simile from physics, heat is the motion of molecules. Too much heat transforms a solid into a liquid and a liquid into the gaseous state, preventing it from assuming any shape. Even in a solid, however, there is a constant "ringing" because the molecules still possess enough energy to vibrate. Only at the temperature of absolute zero does this vibration vanish entirely. The good news is that matter does not have to be cooled all the way down to absolute zero; it can, starting from a few degrees above that, enter a condition called superfluidity or superconductivity, where it begins to exhibit novel and unusual properties. Its hidden potentials, which were previously being dissipated due to that vibration, suddenly become actualized.

We have introduced the basic "subtleties" of the spirit in this chapter—the basic ones being the Heart, the Spirit, the Secret, the Hidden, and the Most Hidden. We observed that the Master invariably counseled self-restraint above all else as the prerequisite for self-development. Chapter 6 now details his essentials of Sufi practice.

6

THE ESSENTIALS OF SUFI PRACTICE

Introduction

In this chapter we shall concentrate on the practical, do-it-yourself aspects of Sufism. Of course, as noted in the previous chapter, some practices can only be performed under the guidance of a qualified master. But authentic Sufi masters are few and far between. Fortunately, because Sufism is based on a churchless religion, there are Sufi methods that one can practice without becoming a member of any hierarchy at all, and even without entering a teacher/student relationship. These methods are inherently safe. They do not present a danger in the way certain others would.

The Three Prerequisites of the Path

Even the tallest building is only as strong as its foundation. If the latter is weak, the building will topple like a house of cards at the slightest tremor.

The Master always said that in order to set out on the way, the seeker needed to fulfill three preconditions. These were a job, a spouse, and faith.

"I ask those who come to me: 'How do you stand as regards a spouse, a job, and faith?' To be dependent on no one. 'When these three are present,' I say, 'you can go on the Path. You can travel the course.'

"A person has faith, his job is fine, but his relationship with his spouse is impaired. Then he still can't travel the Path. This is danger, great danger. He's fine with his faith and spouse, but his financial situation is bad—again, it won't work. It has to be there. But if this tripod is in place, that person can enter the Path. Because he has peace of mind. There's nothing to disturb his peace. May God bestow it on us all.

"Be careful about these three fronts. I tell it to everyone. In time there'll be those who apply to you, tell them the same thing. 'How are you with faith? Can you fulfill God's commandments?' 'Yes.' 'How are you with your spouse?' 'Fine.' 'And with your job?' 'That's okay, too.' Tell them: 'Come to my side.' 'Everything's fine, but not with my spouse.' 'Put that in order, then come.' Spouse and faith are in order, but business is bad: 'Find yourself a job, earn a bite to eat, then come.' Three phases—this is important, this. No matter which one is missing, a person can't enter the Path. He can't travel the course."

The Three Principles of Sufi Sainthood

The Master never tired of explaining that once on the path, there were three principles that needed to be adhered to faithfully. These are abstention from illicit gain, abstention from illicit sex, and performing the Formal Prayer.

Here is a selection, in his own words, of how the Master explained the subject. In one conversation, he started from the three preconditions mentioned above and then went on to say:

"These three points depend on two points. The first is: if you know that the tea I offer you is bought with illicit earnings, don't drink it.

"Don't touch what is prohibited. If you fall victim to hunger and thirst, and there is money by the thousands strewn on the street when you go out, and you're hungry, still don't take it.

"The second is very dangerous. It is worse than the first. You're single. Until you get married, until you marry a suitable woman [or vice versa], everything is ruled out. She can come and sit on your knee, she can stir up your lust beyond endurance, yet you should still see her as your mother or your sister. She is your mother, your sister. One does not engage in lust with one's mother or sister. Even an animal doesn't do it. Don't even eye her. It shouldn't even pass through your mind. She is your sister [or he is your brother].

"Use this, okay? Use this.

"Don't touch what is forbidden even if you were to die of hunger.

"The second is more dangerous. Those who can curb the first can't contain the second. If, outside of marriage, a woman were to come and sit in your lap, if your lust were to boil up, she's your mother, your sister. Don't glance with your eye. Don't even pass it through your mind.

"These are the points that really wreck. Own up to these two points. [Saints like] Hadji Bayram Wali, Rumi, were called saints only when they were able to master these two points to perfection. [The same goes] for all of them.

"You can't find this in books. You won't find *any* of this in any book. This is the crux, these two points. One is, don't look at what is forbidden [in terms of gain or profit], the other is, don't incline towards [illicit] lust. When you promise, come, and the crown of sainthood is yours. But whichever of these you do, it's no use if you were to perform the Formal Prayer or chant invocations day in and day out.

"Whoever pulls in these two brakes—in terms of illicit eating and drinking, and lust—Sainthood will be immediately yours. You might say: 'Uncle, are you crazy?' I'm crazy. Be crazy yourselves, and you'll be the winners.

"Now to summarize, it boils down to the two points I've been telling you. When you're established in these two points, when you do your Five Daily Prayers, when you're with God every instant, that's it.

"Don't eat what is forbidden, don't look at what is forbidden, perform the Formal Prayer. The path consists of these three.

"Formal Prayer is the chief of all worship. The chief.

"Don't give up the Formal Prayer. This is my last will and testament to you."

The Master is gone now, but his advice survives. So if you have any intention of entering the Sufi Path, you have all you need to get started in the Three Prerequisites and Three Principles mentioned above. Measure yourself against the Three Preconditions. If they are fulfilled, you can enter the Path. Then, if you can close the Two Doors and do the Five Daily Prayers (plus maybe a few extra), you will reach the Other Shore sooner or later.

This holds true for all human beings. It was expressed by no less a Friend of God than the Saint of the Age, and it makes no difference that he's physically no longer with us. Further, they are the methods I can recommend without reservation in the absence of a master: everyone can perform them.

Before we go on, please note that *one doesn't have to be a Moslem or a Sufi in order to shut the Two Doors—this is universally beneficial.* We can all become better Buddhists, Christians, Jews, Moslems, etc., by benefitting from this valuable insight of the Master.

Formal Prayer and Fasting

Throughout history, the goal of Enlightenment has been approached through moral behavior, psychospiritual techniques, and worship. The most important worship for the Sufi is the Formal Prayer (Ar. *salat*, Pers. *namaz*), repeated five times daily and totaling approximately forty minutes (at the average rate of a cycle a minute) per day. It is called "Formal" here for lack of a better word, and because it involves a sequence of "forms," or bodily movements. Formal Prayer is so essential that if one wants to be a Moslem or a Sufi without doing it, one shouldn't bother.

Poise. Equilibrium. Calm. Serenity. These are terms that characterize the practitioner of Formal Prayer, for he is in tune with God and with the cosmic rhythms of life. Regarding the Formal Prayer, Alfred Guillaume, himself a Christian, has noted wistfully: ". . . apart from the testimony to Muhammad being the apostle of God there is nothing in the official worship of Islam in which a Christian could not join, and one who understands the words of praise and adoration is tempted to do so."[130] According to Phil Parshall, a Protestant missionary, Moslems are more biblical in their worship than Christians, since the Bible mentions prostration and other positions used by Moslems in Formal Prayer.[131] A person who performs the Prayer properly achieves harmony with God, with the cosmos, with his fellow human beings, and with himself.

But why does the Formal Prayer have any form at all, and this form in particular? We are so accustomed to thinking of the spirit as an abstract principle that we cannot fathom why prayer should be linked to bodily postures.

The reason is that although the spirit itself is far removed from the physical world, it is *coupled to the physical body* via the subtle body. In doing the physical motions, then, what we are doing is moving the spiritual body. It is this movement which, together with the prayers and invocations themselves, serves as an elevator to accomplish the Ascension (thus the Prophet: "Formal Prayer is the Ascension of the faithful"). Once the Ascension is completed, one becomes perfected, and then one's every movement is pure beauty.

Simply for the sake of comparison, it may be instructive to consider Formal Prayer in conjunction with Yoga (Skt. "Union"). Yoga has been traditionally understood as a body of psychophysiological techniques that will, if diligently applied, lead to freedom, liberation, and immortality. As Mircea Eliade has noted, Yoga involves "transforming the human body into a cosmic body."[132] There are many forms of Yoga, the principal geographical versions being Indian, Tibetan, and Chinese Yoga. Yogic techniques have found application in Hinduism, Buddhism, and Zen, not to mention such exotic areas as Taoist alchemy.

We have already seen that man is a mirror of the universe—man is a microcosmos, the universe is a macroanthropos. If this is true, an affinity may be expected to obtain between bodily energies and cosmic energies.[133] The universe is composed of two realms—the physical and the spiritual. From our worldly standpoint, there is no correspondence between the material world of stars and the internal organs of man; hence, the claims of the traditions can hold only in the spiritual realm. It may be conjectured that when human energies are brought into tune with the energies of the cosmos, a "resonance" occurs which allows the ordinary human being to partake in a wider existence. It may be further conjectured that the situation is not black-and-white, that there exist different gradations, different colors or shades of gray, corresponding to different levels of realization between the macro and the micro.

The techniques of Yoga, then, endeavor to fine-tune the body to bring about such a realization, the body here implying not just the physical but also the psychospiritual or "subtle" body. To this end, various approaches are employed, and we shall focus particularly on verbal repetitions (*mantra*), bodily postures (*asana*), control of respiration (*pranayama*), concentration (*dharana*), and meditation (*dhyana*). Moral law is a prerequisite, and some of the Ten Commandments are repeated in the Five Restraints of Yoga.[134]

To begin with *mantras*, the similarities with the Sufic invocation (*dhikr*) have long been recognized.[135] Whereas the *mantra* is generally a nonsense syllable presumed to have mystical significance, however, *dhikr* is the incessant repetition of a Name of God or a sacred formula suffused with divine meaning. In addition, breath-control, concentration, and meditation are combined during Sufic *dhikr*.

The following quote, from an introductory book on Yoga, could have been written by a Sufi: "[E]very man has sooner or later to give birth to his own perfection—in which sense the struggling being of today is the father of his own future perfect self, or perfect man."[136]

Let us now turn to Formal Prayer. What does it consist of? First comes the external requirement of Ablution, which implies both physical cleansing and freshening, and spiritual purification. The basic components of the Formal Prayer are the Opening Proclamation ("God Most Great"), standing with hands clasped (at the waist for men, over the chest for women), genuflection, straightening up, prostration (twice), and sitting on one's heels. All the while, prayers appropriate to each stage are recited.

Photographic plates depicting a sequence similar to the standing, bowing, and straightening postures are to be found in a book dealing with Tibetan wisdom.[137] Although these are techniques of youthfulness and long life, it is interesting that the Tibetans have approached the subject in a ritual mentality. These Yogic postures have to do with transforming and raising energy, which is the true meaning of the Elixir of Life. With each genuflection and prostration, perhaps, energies within the subtle body swirl and are brought into harmony with the energies whirling within the cosmos at large.

But why must it be repeated all life long at the rate of forty cycles per day? If we can regard Formal Prayer as a form of purification, we may compare it to zone melting, or zone refining. This is a process of chemical separation where a ring moving along a cylindrical substance heats the latter to incandescence, and in cooling the substance crystallizes, driving out impurities. This is a highly effective method; the impurities left can be as small as one part in ten billion. These are pushed forward along the rod, and the final action is to nip off the tip where the impurities have become concentrated. On the other hand, zone melting is a very slow process. Not only is the progress of the melting ring slow, but the process has to be repeated until the desired purity is achieved. Because germanium was purified by this method for the transistor, and later on silicon for the integrated circuit, our entire electronics and digital technology depends on it.

Other, more tedious methods of purification are not unknown. The enrichment in a gaseous-diffusion plant of the fissile isotope of uranium, U-235, by separation from its naturally much more abundant but nonfissionable form, U-238, is of this kind. Uranium in the form of uranium hexafluoride is passed from one compartment in a chamber to another through a porous barrier. The resulting enrichment is so slight that the process must be repeated *hundreds of thousands* of times in order to obtain weapons-grade uranium.

In a similar way, Formal Prayer can be considered a slow and painstaking method of spiritual purification, but the results are comparably spectacular if one does the right things long enough. Once the desired level of purity is achieved, the process must be continued, this time in order to *maintain* that ultrapure state. Otherwise, slippages occur.

The prostration and subsequent sitting position are quite reminiscent of the *Yoga Mudra*—literally, "symbol (or binding) of union"—posture in Hatha Yoga. A popular book on this subject notes: "This exercise is extraordinarily beneficial for persons who are inclined to be proud. Pride is driven away from us. We learn to bow humbly before God and to turn to the source of life within us."[138]

What few people realize is that the prostration is also the position of the foetus, and many peoples place their dead in an embryonic position before burial in the hope of securing its rebirth. As an embryonic posture, the prostration signifies the spiritual death-rebirth of the individual. The Saying of the Prophet: "One is closest to God during prostration"—like both a newborn babe and a dead man—is further evidence of this fact.

The Base Self—"the little local self," as Edward Carpenter once called it—fears only three things: hunger, the Formal Prayer, and death. Short of physical death, which would be a cop-out, Fasting and Formal Prayer are therefore the basic methods of taming and transforming the Base Self. This is why people instinctively shy away from these two forms of worship.

The thirty days of Fasting (from dawn to sundown) during the month of Ramadan purify and fine-tune the body to subtle energies at the same time that they subdue the Base Self. Fasting is a time-honored method of purification practiced all over the world. For those who would keep the Base Self under strict control, to eat and drink sparingly is a necessity at other times, too. This leads to light and sparing sleep, with the resulting enhancement in wakefulness, consciousness, and attention. This cannot be maintained on a full stomach, which engenders drowsiness.

Fasting is to refrain, to abstain—and in Sufism it has the further meaning of abstaining from "everything-other-than-God."

Fasting is to refrain from seeing otherness; it is "the presence of the Essence."[139]

Nietzsche's term, "the spirit of gravity," is a good way of describing the Base Self, whose inertia resists any change that might lead to its dissolution. The fear of death is also why, during Formal Prayer, the Base Self can be kept at bay via breath-control.

The Base Self floods the mind with distractions—memories, imaginings, etc.—during Formal Prayer in an effort to nullify its beneficial effects. When breath-control and breath-retention are applied during Formal Prayer, however, the Base Self becomes preoccupied with its own survival, for it interprets the cessation of breathing as a state of emergency. The barrage of distractions it imposes on consciousness is then interrupted, aiding concentration on a fixed point (God) and allowing the performer to derive the maximum benefit from his performance.[140]

The recitation of prayers (mostly from the Book, and in one's own language if otherwise not feasible) allows a person to focus concentration on God and induces a meditative state.[141] The frequent repetition of Names of God during Formal Prayer approximates *dhikr* (invocation).

Thus, it can be seen that *Formal Prayer incorporates all the techniques of Yoga combined*—*mantras* or rather their higher form, *dhikr, asanas* (postures), breath-control, concentration on God, and meditation (*dhyana,* from which Zen is derived) are built into it. In other words, *the single worship of Formal Prayer spans the entire spectrum of Yogic techniques.*

This is not to reduce Formal Prayer to Yoga. *Formal Prayer is not Yoga.* It is a most intimate form of worship, not a psychophysical technique. It combines postures, worship, prayer, concentration, and meditation. Moreover, the Book states that God participates in the Formal Prayer (33:43), in which case it represents *an essential movement of the universe.* But even when measured against the backdrop of Yoga, it can be seen that a whole series of Yogic techniques is implicit in one of the Five Pillars (basic requirements) of Islam.

Moslems do not perform Prayer as a technique, but as a form of worship enjoined upon them by God, seeking His pleasure alone. (Not that God *needs* our Prayer; it's for our own good that Prayer is prescribed for us.) Viewed from a different perspective, however, it becomes obvious that Formal Prayer is the most sophisticated program for spiritual elevation—which is why the Prophet remarked, as we've seen above, that Formal Prayer is the Ascension of the faithful. For the Formal Prayer was enjoined upon believers during the Ascension of the Prophet himself, and it enables them to participate in the energies of that cosmic event.

It turns out, then, that *the "secret method" of the Sufis for spiritual transformation is actually an open secret,* performed by Moslems everywhere, but without cognizance of this possibility. All the other Sufic techniques (dervish dances, etc.) are footnotes to this, supplementary exercises that may support but cannot replace the fundamental requirement.

Up to this point, we have discussed the form of Formal Prayer, because this is its outwardly visible aspect. But what about its content? That content, if all goes well, is the flowering of love—the love of God and, for His sake, the love of His creatures—in the heart of the worshipper. We have already seen the Sacred Tradition: "I was a hidden treasure, and . . . created the universe . . . through love."

The Turkish Sufi poet Yunus observed that "Love is a long syllable." Just how long is explained by another Sufi poet, Fuzuli: "Whatever exists in the universe is love." This means that the entire cosmos is woven out of love. If one performs his Formal Prayers properly, the realization of this truth will gradually dawn on a person, and he will finally become suffused with, and engulfed in, love. He will thus be practicing Bhakti Yoga, the

Yoga of Love. This will lead to Divine Attraction and Gnosis, or experiential Knowledge of God, and the practitioner will be engaging in Jnana Yoga, the Yoga of Knowledge. It can be seen, then, that Formal Prayer runs across a whole range of Yogic practices.

The Symbolic Meaning of Prayer

For the Sufis, every stage of the Formal Prayer has its symbolic meaning. The Ablution, which is purification done with pure water, has its spiritual counterpart in the "water of the unseen," dispensed from the Hearts of Gnostics. The purpose is to cleanse the self of impurities (everything other than God, connections with the world) simultaneously with bodily purification.

In the Sufic conception, Prayer is the link between the servant of God and his Lord. Ideally, it is Arrival. Standing is the courtesy of Formal Prayer—ideally, Extinction (*fana*). Clasping the hands is contraction—one becomes "gathered" (*jam*) and draws closer to "the Real" (*Haqq*: Ultimate Reality or God). Recitation is speech; Sufis call it "conversation with God." Bowing is the Unification of Acts and Attributes. More precisely, it is the effacement of these from oneself as well as from "everything-other-than-God," and dedicating them to their true source, who is God. Straightening up is ideally performed by the Lord, not by the servant.

The first prostration is the Unification of the Essence, at which point Annihilation from existence is experienced. The performer annihilates himself from everything-other-than-God. The second prostration is the Annihilation from Annihilation (the "negation of the negation"). The performer rises from it, reborn in Continuation (*baqa*). Henceforth, his existence is with his Lord.

Saluting the right and the left by saying "Peace" at the end of the Prayer is to return to creation, to normal everyday life, after the servant has been in the Presence of the Supreme Ultimate (his Lord). Existence becomes confirmed again in his sight.[142]

Needless to say, this is the Prayer only of the accomplished Gnostic. But every Formal Prayer is a preparation for that accomplishment. The processes that elevate a person, resulting ultimately in Arrival, occur largely in the subconscious. But no matter how unconscious they may be, these processes lead a servant towards his Lord as surely as the world turns even though we cannot feel it.

Many, many repetitions are necessary before one can achieve Arrival. Just how many depends on numerous things. It may involve lifelong effort, and even this may not be enough—but in that case, the elevation serves its purpose in the Afterlife. And even one who has "Arrived" must continue to do the Prayer, because such is the command of his Lord. He continues to perform the Formal Prayer both to maintain his Realization and as an example to other people.

A Place in the Sun

God has given man everything—has exalted him above all else—but He has not given him His Divinity, His Godhood. As the Prophet of God said, the highest station is the station of being a servant of God. The Book counsels us to "call on Him humbly, with fear and longing" (7:55-56). Obedience to God and humility are man's best tools on this path.

The Perfect Man is not God. He is, rather, the viceregent of God on Earth. As such, although he is a human being, and although there is little to distinguish him from other people in his outward appearance, in his inner, spiritual life he is invested with exceptional qualities that set him apart from ordinary human beings. These superior qualities are in principle available to all ordinary mortals by virtue of their being human (though some may be more gifted than others). The Perfect Human differs from others only in that he has undergone special training to enhance or develop these qualities, endured the hardships of the Way, and emerged triumphantly on the far shore of Realization.

For example, the Book states of the prophet Idris: "We raised him to a lofty station" (19:57). Sometimes identified with Enoch, Idris is also confused with Hermes, due to the similarity between the spectacular heavenly journeys experienced by the two.

The great Sufi sage Ibn Arabi has explained in *The Bezels of Wisdom* that Idris and Noah were both raised to the sphere of the sun. In classical astronomy, the nine principal spheres denoted a series of nested, concentric, transparent spheres surrounding the Earth, on which the orbit of each heavenly body resided. Before we dismiss these as fantasies of the ancients, however, we might pause to consider the possibility that these spheres can also be taken to mean something quite in accord with modern astronomy—namely, the spheroid shapes of the heavenly bodies themselves. "The sphere of the sun" can then be understood as "the sun disk," or simply "the sun." Noah's and Idris' Ascension to and their establishment in the sun must have a very profound meaning in terms of the relationship between man and cosmos, yet its exact meaning escapes us, and in such a case silence is preferable to misleading speculation. Still, we should strive to get out of the walnut-shell of our brains and take (spiritual) wing to the Milky Way.

<hr/>

This chapter has described the essentials of Sufi practice according to the Master: a job, a spouse, and faith in God; abstention from illicit gain and illicit sexual relations; along with attentive performance of the Formal Prayer and Fasting. The full significance of the Formal Prayer was explored. We concluded by observing that man should open himself to the universe, not just physically but spiritually. Chapter 7 now explores questions related to society and Sufism.

7

THE SATANIC VERSES AND THE DEMOCRATIC PERSONALITY

Untime of the Imam

Loose-robed, frowning, ominous, awake: this is the Imam.
. . . The Imam is a massive stillness, an immobility. His
great gnarled hands, granite-grey, rest heavily on the wings
of his high-backed chair. . . .

"We will make a revolution," the Imam proclaims, . . .
"that is a revolt not only against a tyrant, but against history." For there is an enemy beyond Ayesha, and that is
History herself. . . . History is a deviation from the Path,
knowledge is a delusion. . . . "We will unmake the veil of
history . . . and when it is unravelled, we will see Paradise
standing there, in all its glory and light. . . . We seek the
eternity, the timelessness of God."

. . . [T]he Imam . . . hoists up his skirts to reveal
two spindly legs with an almost monstrous covering of
hair . . . and settles on Gibreel's shoulders, clutching on to
him with fingernails that have grown into long, curved
claws. Gibreel feels himself rising into the sky, bearing the

old man of the sea, the Imam with hair that grows longer by the minute, streaming in every direction, his eyebrows like pennants in the wind. . . .

"They [the people] love me," the Imam's voice says, ". . . They love me for my habit of smashing clocks. . . . We long for the eternal, and I am eternity. . . . After the revolution there will be no clocks; we'll smash the lot. . . . After the revolution there will be no birthdays. We shall all be born again, all of us the same unchanging age in the eye of Almighty God."

. . . And Gibreel . . . sees the Imam grown monstrous, lying in the palace forecourt with his mouth yawning open at the gates; as the people march through the gates he swallows them whole.

[It is] the end of time, the hour that is beyond measuring, the hour of . . . the commencement of the Untime of the Imam.[143]

When Ayatollah Khomeini passed the death sentence on Salman Rushdie, was he under the influence of these words? Had he read those passages? Was he aware of them? For the reference is painfully obvious. Whether the Imam had read the book or not, for once he succeeded in rallying behind him the world of Islam, which found much cause in Rushdie's book for grievance.

Post-Nietzsche, ours is a strangely iconoclastic age. Nothing is sacred any more. Far beyond that, "respect" has almost become a taboo word. The ridicule of exaltation and the exaltation of ridicule has become the rule. For example, some people claim that Jesus was a homosexual, and a bishop claimed that the Virgin Mary was a prostitute. But not everyone shares this attitude. Such a declaration is deeply injurious not only to sincere Christians, but also to Moslems, who consider Jesus to be among the most eminent of prophets, and hold Mary in great reverence.

Likewise, any insinuation against Moses would be deeply offensive—and, because Moslems embrace all earlier prophets, ditto for any others.

It is not my intention here to subject *The Satanic Verses* to a detailed analysis. Many years have passed. The Imam died shortly afterwards, and Rushdie has gained his freedom. What I want to focus on instead is the excerpt above. Rushdie appears to have had an insight into the Imam's mentality, for he is here equating *qiyam* (uprising, revolt) with *qiyamah* (Resurrection, Judgment Day). In Rushdie's reading of the Imam's motivations, the apocalyptic metamorphoses into the secular, the eschatological into the temporal. The revolution will put an end to history, to time, and we shall stand in the eternity of God's Paradise.

Even if this confusion actually occurred in the Imam's mind, however, the fact remains that the Revolution was not, is not, and can never be the Day of Resurrection. It was not the end of history; rather, it has become a part of history, slightly fraying at the edges now that Iran's youth have demonstrated their protest. The mullahs themselves are of two minds, one faction clinging to the political authority established by Khomeini, while another contends that the whole involvement of the Iranian clergy in politics was a big mistake right from the beginning.[144]

Ah, the Iranian clergy. Now *there* is an interesting turn of phrase. For the notion of a church, of a clerical body of holy men dictating orthodox belief, is wholly alien to the essence of Islam. How did we get from the initial Islamic proto-community to Khomeini's doctrine, "government of the jurisconsult" (*valayat al-faqih*), who is the highest politico-religious authority in Iran, fourteen centuries later?

It's a long and complicated story, and I do not intend to go into the details. Bernard Lewis, the noted historian of the Middle East, summed up the result as follows: "Khomeini during his rule seems to have effected a kind of 'Christianization' of Iran's Islamic institutions, with himself as an infallible pope, and with the functional equivalent of a hierarchy of archbishops, bishops, and priests. All of this was totally alien to Islamic tradition, and thus constituted an 'Islamic revolution' in a sense quite different from the one usually conveyed by references to Khomeini's legacy."[145] In *The Middle East* (1995), Professor Lewis stated that Iran's Islamic Revolution had more to do with the French and Russian Revolutions than with Islam, and more in common with Robespierre and Stalin than with Mohammed or Ali; its methods were revolutionary, not Islamic. Outside Iran, those methods found echo in a marginal minority sharing the same generic personality type (about which more will follow).

Material vs. Spiritual Knowledge

Setting aside those aspects of Rushdie's treatment that were downright offensive to Moslems, there are two questions he raises that merit serious interest. The first problem is, at root, epistemological, the second political. Let us look at the epistemological issue before proceeding to the latter.

The question is whether Revelation negates all other forms of knowledge. If the answer is yes, the consequences are as Rushdie describes them. One then comes to view the crowning achievements of civilization as "the greatest of the lies—progress, science, rights . . . knowledge is a delusion, because the sum of knowledge was complete on the day [God] finished his revelation to the [Prophet]. . . . Burn the books and trust the Book, shred the papers and hear the Word. . . ."[146]

Does knowledge of the Other World, the Afterworld, contradict knowledge of this world? Does knowledge of the spiritual world cancel knowledge of the physical world? If we reflect for a moment, we shall see that this is the mirror image of our position—for we have assumed exactly the opposite. Contemporary mentality, if not modern science itself, is firmly rooted in the conviction that knowledge of the physical world renders spiritual knowledge void.

Both positions are halfway houses. A truly holistic epistemology would start from the premise that both forms of knowledge complement and complete each other. And it is here that a saying attributed to the Prophet assumes paramount importance: "Science is two sciences [i.e. of two kinds]: first, the science of bodies [physical/secular science], and then the science of religions [spiritual/sacred science]." Note carefully that the Prophet puts physical knowledge first, *despite the fact that he is the founder of a world religion;* it is knowledge of our external world that must take precedence over subtler matters. But we have now succeeded in gaining knowledge about the material world, beyond the dreams of all previous civilizations. What remains is to complete this by devoting attention to the spiritual world, *but without sacrificing our hard-earned physical knowledge.* Spiritual knowledge is perhaps a trifle less urgent, but on a higher level, because the Prophet assigns it second place. Only after the fundamental physical needs and the need for physical knowledge are satisfied can one deal with higher matters (incidentally in accordance with psychologist Abraham Maslow's hierarchy of needs).

God is the Omniscient (*al-Alim*) and the Designer, the Inventor, the Great Architect or Engineer of the universe. As such, He is the fount of all knowledge, no matter of what kind. A thousand years ago, Moslem countries laid the foundation of the first scientific civilization on the perception that to know more about God's creation is, simultaneously, to know more about God, His intentions, and His method. This is entirely in line with the Prophet's advice to "Seek knowledge, even if it be in China"— obviously any knowledge to be found in China would have little to do directly with Revelation. Book-burning was anathema, because of the stance that "All books are explanations of and extended commentaries on the Book." Indeed, every creature, even the whole of nature, was a sign/verse (*ayah*) from God, and hence worthy of reverent study if not itself actually sacred.

But this exquisite balance could not be maintained for long. The East grew increasingly static on the assumption that true (spiritual) knowledge, i.e. Revelation, was complete, while the West grew increasingly dynamic, moving from one mental revolution to another in its incessant search for physical knowledge. The West has been preoccupied with form, the East with content or meaning. But once we perceive that appearance and content, form and meaning, phenomenon and noumenon, matter and spirit, cannot be divorced from each other but are instead inextricably bound—form arising as a manifestation of meaning—then we can never accept a regression to partial approaches. For phenomenon is noumenon congealed.

Picture what would happen if both viewpoints were accepted. We would continue to have material well-being, but psychological and spiritual well-being would now complement this. We would be able to make the best of both worlds. Greater compassion would result in a more equitable distribution of global wealth, which in turn would result in a more secure and peaceable world. The dichotomy between static and dynamic would be resolved into stable change, or change through continuity. No great rifts would remain, or appear, between mind and heart, between spirit and body. Our ailing civilization would be healed. Further, the points of contact between spiritual and physical knowledge would lead to the emergence of a third, and for us entirely new, kind of knowledge—what is called "hidden knowledge" (*ilm al-ladun*) in Sufism.

And let me let you in on a little secret. Even if we can't achieve this collectively, it can still be realized individually. Our own lives will be enriched, to the extent that we ourselves are able to implement the requirements of this healing vision.

The Political Dimension

Islam is a religion. It is not a political ideology, and it is not primarily interested in politics. The Book does not prescribe any sort of political regime as preferable over any other. Yet there is a way in which Islam does impinge on politics. That way is rather different than what the regimes found in latter-day (pseudo-)Islamic countries would lead one to expect.

Apparently, not much constructive thinking has been devoted to political thinking in Islam in recent centuries. Yet I want to suggest that the insights of Sufism can be harnessed to provide a fresh and novel contribution to social and political thought.

Contrary to widespread opinion, there are no irresolvable contradictions between Islam and secular life. One verse from the Book: "There is no coercion in religion" (2:256), and one saying of the Prophet: "There is no clergy/monasticism in religion," ensure that Islam does not advocate theocracy, although in some cases, people have found ways of ushering it in through the back door. The verse affirms freedom of religion, while the saying explains why there is no church in Islam. The mosque is simply a building of worship, not a religious organization or institution.

The Ottomans were probably the best example of religious tolerance and pluralism in the past, and during the persecution of Jews in the Spanish reign of Ferdinand and Isabella, the Ottoman Empire provided safe haven for all the refugees. Israelis who have migrated from Turkey invariably have fond memories of their earlier lives there. (We should never forget that the Arab-Israeli conflict arose from a political and geographical, not a religious, dispute.)

Throughout history, the religion has found a mode of living with the powers that be, compromising where necessary, not interfering with rulers beyond a certain point. Its resilience has enabled it to survive under a variety of regimes. The question, however, of what kind of political system Islam would naturally correspond to has seldom been raised. I wish to do so here.

Let us first lend ear to a sympathetic critic. It may be best to let Professor Bernard Lewis speak for himself:

> [W]e can discern elements in Islamic law and tradition that could assist the development of one or another form of democracy. . . .
>
> Islamic tradition strongly disapproves of arbitrary rule. The central institution of sovereignty in the traditional Islamic world, the caliphate, is defined by . . . features that distinguish caliphs from despots. The exercise of political power is conceived and presented as a contract, creating bonds of mutual obligation between the ruler and the ruled. Subjects are duty-bound to obey the ruler and carry out his orders, but the ruler also has duties towards the subject, similar to those set forth in most cultures.
>
> The contract can be dissolved if the ruler fails to fulfill or ceases to be capable of fulfilling his obligations. Although rare, there have been instances when such dissolutions took place. There is, therefore, also an element of consent in the traditional Islamic view of government.
>
> [In spite] of what has actually happened [in history,] the central point remains: there are elements in Islamic culture that could favor the development of democratic institutions.
>
> [According to a saying of the Prophet,] diversity is something to be welcomed, not something to be suppressed. This attitude is typified by the acceptance . . . of four different schools of Islamic jurisprudence. . . . The idea that it is possible to be orthodox even while differing creates a

principle of the acceptance of diversity and of mutual tolerance of differences of opinion that surely cannot be bad for parliamentary government.

The final point worth mentioning . . . is Islam's emphasis on the twin qualities of dignity and humility. Subjects—even the humblest subjects—have personal dignity in the traditional Islamic view, and rulers must avoid arrogance.[147]

Democracy and Ethics

It is well known, of course, that the concept of democracy first flourished in ancient Greece. I want to look at the first principles, shared even by an antidemocrat such as Plato or a moderate critic like Aristotle, that guided the Greeks in building the framework for democracy. Professor Robert A. Dahl has neatly summarized these assumptions:

> [O]nly in association with others can we hope to become fully human or, certainly, to realize our qualities of excellence as human beings . . . it is our nature to be social beings. . . . Nothing is more important in judging the quality of a city [polis] than the qualities of excellence it fosters in its citizens . . . a good city is one that produces good citizens, promotes their happiness, and encourages them to act rightly . . . these ends are harmonious; for the virtuous man will be a happy man, and no one . . . can be truly happy unless he is also virtuous.
>
> So it is also with justice. Virtue, justice, and happiness are not enemies but companions. Since justice is what tends to promote the common interest, a good polis must also be just; and therefore it must aim at developing citizens who seek the common good. For one who merely pursues

his own interest cannot be a good citizen: a good citizen is one who in public matters aims always at the common good . . . in public matters he looks always to the good of the polis.

. . . [I]n the best polis, citizens are at once virtuous, just, and happy. And because each seeks the good of all, and the city is not divided into smaller cities of rich and poor, or of different gods, all citizens can live together in harmony.[148]

From this summary, we are enabled to make two observations. One is that the underpinnings of democracy involve, above all, an ethical approach, and wherever there is ethics, religions have usually not been far behind. The second is the emphasis on excellence in human beings, which links directly to the concept of the Perfect Human in Sufism. If human perfection is a goal to be sought after, Sufism and democracy share a single aim.

Now when the scholars of Islam first encountered the remnants of Greek civilization, they found much therein—with the exception of polytheism and a few other things—that was close to their hearts. (The Sufi Abdulqarim Jili, author of *The Perfect Human,* was not alone in considering Plato the sage of Greece.) Their efforts to translate Greek texts into Arabic, to which we owe our own awareness of ancient Greek culture, was not, for them, an exercise in futility.

Thus when al-Farabi, the famous Islamic scholar, put pen to paper more than a thousand years ago in order to analyze "Virtuous Government" or "the Perfect State" (*al-madina al-fadila*),[149] his ideas were not far different from what we have seen above:

In order to preserve himself and to attain his highest perfections every human being is by his very nature in need of many things which he cannot provide all by himself; he is indeed in need of people who each supply him with some particular need of his. Everybody finds himself in the same relation to everybody in this respect. Therefore man cannot attain the perfection, for the sake of which his inborn nature has been given to him, unless many (societies of) people who co-operate come together who each supply everybody else with some particular need of his, so that as a result of the contribution of the whole community all the things are brought together which everybody needs in order to preserve himself and to attain perfection. . . . The most excellent good and the utmost perfection is, in the first instance, attained in a city [*madina*], not in a society which is less complete than it.[150]

Farabi believed that the perfect state, ruled by a philosopher-prophet-king, is based on true justice and proportionate equality. While he did not believe that democracy itself was that state, he claimed elsewhere that the "democratic city" was the best breeding ground for the perfect state: "In the 'democratic' state all sorts of desires and ways of behaviour come together. Therefore it is not impossible that in the course of time excellent men should grow up in it, and that wise men, orators and poets should exist in it. . . .Thus it would become possible to gather from its parts for the Perfect State. This is one of the good things which arise in this state." Furthermore, he adds: "[I]t is more possible and easier to set up perfect states and the rule of excellent men from . . . 'democratic states'. . . ."[151] Farabi seems to have regarded democracy as a precursor of ideal government.

Our discussion so far suggests that democracy has at bottom to do with ethics, and only secondarily with free elections in a multiparty system. If this is true, one could envisage alternative (and perhaps even better) possibilities for democratic development. It is the "spirit of democracy" that is really essential, and this spirit has a lot to do with the ethical assumptions in the minds of people. From this, it stands to reason that cultivating certain traits in human beings will be more conducive to the flowering of democracy, even if this political outcome is not explicitly achieved.

From Civility to Courtesy

The social sciences of the past century have devoted much effort to the understanding of democracy versus totalitarianism, and how to avoid the latter outcome. One such study was conducted by Theodor W. Adorno and his associates throughout most of the 1940s, published under the title *The Authoritarian Personality* (1950). Here, a scale was devised for distinguishing between two types of human personality: authoritarian and democratic. Today, it is more or less accepted that the main characteristics of the authoritarian personality are: rigidity in views, hostility, fear of anarchy and change, obedience to strong centralized authority, and a repressive attitude towards inferiors. Characteristics of the democratic personality include tolerance of differing views, ability and flexibility in reaching a compromise, and adaptiveness to change.

When viewed on this scale, Sufis emerge as past masters of flexibility and resilience. In many teaching stories, they overcome an obstacle set by the powers that be through the creative exercise of intelligence. One such story (apparently a historical event) that immediately comes to mind is the case of Ahmed Sirhindi (also known as Imam Rabbani).

WHEN A SULTAN FORCED HIM TO PASS THROUGH A LOW GATEWAY IN AN EFFORT TO HAVE THE MASTER BOW BEFORE HIM, THE IMAM, WHO MADE IT A POINT NOT TO BOW DOWN BEFORE ANYTHING EXCEPT GOD, WENT THROUGH ON HIS KNEES, BUT WITH HEAD HELD HIGH AND HIS BODY ERECT.

The idea that a certain kind of society breeds a specific human type goes back a long way. Plato discussed the type of human being that democracies engender in *The Republic* (555b-562a). Plato wasn't a fan of democracy; he advocated Philosopher Kings. (Which wouldn't be such a bad idea, except that they're so hard to come by in real life. How many philosopher kings do you remember from history?) Hence, he dwells on the more dubious aspects of democratic personality: rugged individualism, self-centeredness, license instead of freedom, self-aggrandizement.

But of course, these are not the only characteristics of democratic personalities or societies. Social scientists such as Samuel Huntington, Alex Inkeles, and Friedrich Hayek have outlined the conditions of "civility," a prime trait of the democratic personality structure. Among these are: 1. Cordial, trustful relationships between strangers; 2. Moral, even sacred, performance of the political center; 3. Compassion; 4. The ruler's accountability to the people, which is linked to: 5. Legality; 6. An open and free marketplace in a) economic, b) intellectual, and c) political terms.[152]

Now these are all traits that are current among the Sufis, and in fact can be found among the general populace wherever Islam is lived properly. Cordiality and trust, plus compassion, are properties that any Sufi on the path leading to Perfect Humanity must cultivate. Legality is characteristic of Islamic societies. Bernard Lewis has explained how "the rights of the people" in the West translates into "the duties of the ruler" in Islam. Perhaps the most problematic propositions are Items 2 and 6.c, yet even here, a truly God-fearing ruler would be duty-bound to abstain from immoral action.

Civility reaches its summit in courtesy or sublime conduct (*adab*), perhaps the single most indispensable requirement of Sufism. Hence, if democracy calls for a democratic personality structure, and the latter calls for civility, it is in Sufism that both find their culmination. This reminds me of another Sufi teaching story extolling humility, harmony, and altruism—all aspects of courtesy. Although only the last part of it is really germane to our discussion, I can't resist relating it in full.

A CERTAIN RULER WAS ONE DAY MADE AWARE OF THE EXISTENCE OF THE PEOPLE OF WISDOM. THE SULTAN HAD NOT HEARD OF THEM BEFORE. HE ASKED HIS VIZIER, WHO WAS HIGHLY INTELLIGENT AND HIS GUIDE IN ALL MATTERS, "WHAT IS THE DIFFERENCE BETWEEN A MAN OF KNOWL-EDGE AND A MAN OF WISDOM, A SCHOLAR AND A SUFI, A SCIENTIST AND A SAGE?"

"YOUR HIGHNESS," SAID THE VIZIER, "THIS IS BEST EXPLAINED BY WATCHING THE RESPECTIVE GROUPS IN ACTION." SO THEY FIRST WENT TO A SYMPOSIUM OF SCHOLARS AND SCIENTISTS—DRESSED UP INCOGNITO, OF COURSE. THEY STATIONED THEMSELVES AT THE ENTRANCE. "OBSERVE, YOUR HIGHNESS," SAID THE VIZIER.

AS THE WORTHIES, EACH AN INTELLECTUAL GIANT IN HIS OWN RIGHT, BEGAN TO COME IN, THE VIZIER ASKED THE FIRST ONE: "WHO IS THE GREATEST AMONG YOU?" "I AM, OF COURSE," CAME THE REPLY. "ME, NATU-RALLY," SAID THE SECOND. THE SAME QUESTION WAS ASKED, AND THE SAME REPLY RECEIVED, FROM ALL PARTICIPANTS IN THE SYMPOSIUM.

"NOW, YOUR HIGHNESS," SAID THE VIZIER, "LET US GO TO A SUFI CON-VENTION." SIMILAR SCENE, DIFFERENT PEOPLE, AND THE VIZIER ADDRESSED THE SAME QUESTION TO THE FIRST ENTRANT.

"BEHIND ME," HE ANSWERED, AND HURRIED IN. THE SECOND SAGE GAVE THE SAME REPLY. SO DID THE THIRD, AND THE FOURTH . . . UNTIL THE LAST ONE, WHO SAID, "THEY ALL WENT IN BEFORE ME."

"LET US COME BACK IN THE EVENING, WHEN THEY'RE ALL ABOUT TO DISPERSE," SAID THE VIZIER. NOW BOTH THE SYMPOSIUM AND THE CON-VENTION WERE OCCURRING IN BUILDINGS CLOSE TO EACH OTHER, AND THERE WAS A RIVER FLOWING IN FRONT OF BOTH—A SHALLOW RIVER

WITH STONES IN IT. THE VIZIER GAVE INSTRUCTIONS SO THAT OTHER ROADS WOULD BE BLOCKED, AND BOTH THE SCIENTISTS AND THE SAGES WOULD BE FORCED TO CROSS THE RIVER.

"WATCH," HE TOLD THE SULTAN.

THE MEN OF KNOWLEDGE WERE THE FIRST TO LEAVE. SEEING THAT THERE WAS NOWHERE ELSE TO GO, THEY ALL TACKLED THE RIVER, EACH IN HIS OWN HAPHAZARD WAY. THEY SHOULDERED EACH OTHER, THERE WAS ROUGH PLAY, PANDEMONIUM REIGNED. SHOUTS WERE HEARD, SOME STUMBLED AND WET THEIR GARMENTS, WHILE OTHERS EVEN FELL INTO THE RIVER.

THE VIZIER SMILED. "LET'S HURRY OVER TO THE CONVENTION," HE SAID TO THE SULTAN.

THEY ARRIVED JUST IN TIME TO SEE THE FIRST SAGE EMERGE. IMMEDIATELY TAKING IN THE SITUATION, HE SAID TO THE FELLOW BEHIND HIM: "FOLLOW IN MY EXACT FOOTSTEPS," AND PROCEEDED ACROSS THE RIVER, USING THE ROCKS AS STEPPING STONES. AND SO DID ALL THE REST, CAREFULLY USING ONLY THE STONES STEPPED ON BY THEIR PREDECESSOR. THEY WERE ACROSS THE RIVER IN NO TIME; NOT EVEN THEIR SHOES WERE WET.

"FOR OUR ENCORE, YOUR MAJESTY," SAID THE VIZIER, "WE SHALL HAVE TO MAKE SPECIAL ARRANGEMENTS. AND WE SHALL HAVE TO INVITE YOUR SUBJECTS TO DINNER." HE GAVE ORDERS FOR SPECIAL SPOONS TO BE MADE.

A FEW DAYS LATER, BOTH GROUPS RECEIVED INVITATIONS FROM THE PALACE TO HAVE SUPPER. IT WAS ARRANGED SO THAT ONE GROUP WOULD ARRIVE EARLIER THE SAME EVENING, THE OTHER LATER.

THE SCIENTISTS ARRIVED FIRST AND WERE USHERED INTO THE DINING ROOM.

WHAT THEY SAW WAS THIS: A ROUND TABLE, IN THE CENTER A POT OF SOUP, AND SPOONS SET UP AROUND THE TABLE—SPOONS WITH A HANDLE AT LEAST A YARD LONG.

DOUBTFUL AS TO HOW TO PROCEED, THEY TOOK THEIR SEATS AROUND THE TABLE. BUT WHEN THEY TRIED TO EAT, THEY FOUND IT TO BE IMPOSSIBLE. THE SPOONS WERE TOO LONG TO BE HELD CONVENIENTLY, AND IF

THEY TRIED TO HOLD ONE AT A SHORTER LENGTH, ITS TIP WOULD INTRUDE INTO THE EYE OF A NEIGHBOR. THERE WAS A GREAT COMMOTION AS THE SOUP WAS SPILLED ALL OVER THE TABLE, TO THE ACCOMPANIMENT OF SHOUTS: "WATCH OUT!" "OUCH!" AND "I'LL SHOW YOU!" FINALLY THEY WENT AWAY, HUNGRY, MALCONTENT, AND GRUMBLING AT EACH OTHER.

NEXT IT WAS THE SAGES' TURN. THEY ARRIVED, SAT THEMSELVES AROUND THE TABLE, TOOK UP THE SPOONS—AND BEGAN TO FEED EACH OTHER, EACH PERSON DIPPING A SPOON INTO THE SOUP AND THEN OFFERING IT TO THE PERSON DIRECTLY ACROSS THE TABLE. THE SPOONS, IT TURNED OUT, WERE MADE EXACTLY THE RIGHT LENGTH FOR JUST THIS APPROACH. THEY ALL SUPPED IN QUIET MERRIMENT, THANKED THE SULTAN AND THE VIZIER, AND DEPARTED IN DECORUM.

"THAT," OBSERVED THE VIZIER TO THE SULTAN, "IS THE DIFFERENCE BETWEEN A MAN OF MERE KNOWLEDGE AND A MAN WHO IS TRULY WISE, THE DIFFERENCE BETWEEN A SCHOLAR AND A SAGE."

Monotheism and Equality

One of the root concepts of democracy is that all men and women are created equal. The last part of this statement, however, is incomplete. For if we wish to be accurate historically, we should have to say that all men are equal *before God*. Professor Dahl explains why democracy really came into its own in a monotheistic culture in recent history:

> . . . [D]emocracy might, like Plato's republic, be little more than a philosophical fantasy were it not for the persistent and widespread influence of the belief that human beings are intrinsically equal in a fundamental way—or at any rate some substantial group of human beings are. Historically, the idea of intrinsic equality gained much of its strength, particularly in Europe and the English-speaking countries, from the common doctrine of Judaism and

Christianity (shared also by Islam) that we are equally God's children [or servants]. Indeed it was exactly on this belief that Locke grounded his assertion of the natural equality of all persons in a state of nature.[153]

It is a core Islamic belief that all human beings, whether they share one's faith or not, are one's equals in creation, descended from the same ancestors (Adam and Eve). One day, when a funeral was passing by, the Prophet stood up in respect. His Companions informed him: "That man was a Jew." He replied: "He was a human being, wasn't he?" Since, moreover, one's inner condition at the last moment can never be known for sure, it is best to reserve judgment about others with regard to both the past and the future.

The Open Society

Closely linked with civility and human rights is the concept of an open society. Financier and social philosopher George Soros explains:

> The term "open society" was coined by Henri Bergson, in his book *The Two Sources of Morality and Religion* (1932), and given greater currency by the Austrian philosopher Karl Popper, in his book *The Open Society and Its Enemies* (1945). Popper showed that totalitarian ideologies like communism and Nazism have a common element: they claim to be in possession of the ultimate truth. Since the ultimate truth is beyond the reach of humankind, these ideologies have to resort to oppression in order to impose their vision on society. Popper juxtaposed with these totalitarian ideologies another view of society, which recognizes that nobody has a monopoly on

the truth; different people have different views and different interests, and there is a need for institutions that allow them to live together in peace. These institutions protect the rights of citizens and ensure freedom of choice and freedom of speech. Popper called this form of social organization the "open society."[154]

There is room enough in God's universe for plurality of every imaginable kind: for trees and birds and stars and worms. The entire universe is an open society. ("If your Lord had wanted, He could have made all humankind one single community"— 11:118.) If we wish to adopt the ethics of God, as Sufism prescribes, we should face all His creatures with the same benevolence. Absolute Reality deliberately created endless diversity, and if anyone claiming to possess the ultimate truth is incapable of tolerating differing views, this has nothing to do with ultimate truth, but with our old adversary, the Base Self. This also indicates that if Islamic thinkers and rulers had paid more attention to the principles of Sufism, they might have been able to derive a theory of democracy quite independently.

Everybody worships God as He is seen through the filter of one's own conceptions, but Ultimate Reality is beyond them all and not limited to any filtered image. Hence, any claim to knowledge of the ultimate truth must be redressed by a corrective factor that is best self-administered. Only in a theocracy can people claim to think and speak in God's name, something which even the Prophet didn't do ("I am just a human being like you, just a warner"), and only in an ideocracy can they do the same in the name of some ideology. If one concentrates one's attention on overcoming one's own failings rather than on how to lord it over others, one reaches a more desirable state. As the Ottoman poet Ziya Pasha remarked:

Those who would order the world with their words
There are a thousand kinds of negligence in their own houses.

It was such a refined sensibility—embodied in the *millet*
(nation) system—that allowed the Ottomans to rule in the
Balkans and elsewhere for hundreds of years, with the diverse
communities coexisting peacefully. (Look at the Balkans now.)
American democracy is informed, at least in spirit, with the liberal tolerance of the Ottomans towards diverse religious "nations."

The question arises: if Islam and Sufism were so conducive to
democracy, how come Islamic societies proved so incapable of
developing democracy within themselves? One reason is that in
historical terms, democracy in the modern sense is a compara-
tively recent phenomenon, even in the West—its history does not
go back much further than a couple of centuries. Another reason
is that authoritarian personalities, having once seized political
power, cling to it and are reluctant to share it with others. There
are other reasons as well; the two I have mentioned appear sufficiently explanatory.

The Nemesis of Democracy

I believe enough has been said to convince even the most
hard-boiled skeptic that, whatever the facts of history and of the
more recent past, democracy has an ally in Islamic Sufism.

The Master opposed the Soviet Union "because," he said, "it
is a dictatorship." But while he approved of democracy, he found
two serious flaws with it. "These flaws," he said, "will result in
the downfall not merely of democracy but also, if they go
unremedied, of all humankind." It was not simply that he agreed
with Plato about how freedom breeds license, how people abuse
freedom. Nor was it simply a question of the needless dissent,

even enmity, engendered by the existence of multiple political parties. Far more grave and ultimately fatal, in his view, were unchecked self-interest and extramarital sex. These two fed on each other and made an extremely explosive combination that would sooner or later end in disaster.

If we know the path that leads to calamity, we can deduce the path that leads to salvation. What we earlier saw on the individual, personal level now confronts us on the social level: if we can protect ourselves against illicit gain and illicit sex, we shall have given democracy a lasting lease on life. A doctor of the Master's circle once made a telling observation in connection with biotechnology and genetic manipulation: "There are limits in the macrocosmos, as there are limits in the microcosmos, which man must not transgress." By taking what does not belong to us on a planet with finite resources, and by coveting our own boundless gratification, we do others a great wrong. But as we have already seen in Chapter 2, in reality there are no others, so we shall ourselves ultimately suffer for that wrong.

World Poverty: A Sufi Proposal

Recalling that "whatever we do, we do to ourselves," I would like to conclude this chapter—devoted largely to social issues—by suggesting both a solution to world poverty *and* a boost for democracy, from the standpoint of Islamic Sufism.

As George Soros notes, "an open society may also be threatened . . . from excessive individualism. Too much competition and too little cooperation can cause intolerable inequities and instability. . . . Unless it is tempered by the recognition of a common interest that ought to take precedence over particular interests, our present system—which, however imperfect, qualifies as an open society—is liable to break down."[155] If, together with Soros, we wish to achieve a global open society, here's how it can be done. This involves a novel application of the alms-tax concept, which is a special form of charity.

The beginning of the twenty-first century finds the world with a population in excess of six billion, among whom there exists a tremendous imbalance between rich and poor. The world's three richest men command an income equal to the total income of 600 million human beings living in poor countries. The 225 richest people in the world,[156] or the 400 richest people in the United States alone,[157] possess a combined wealth of more than $1 trillion—equal to the annual incomes of the poorest 2.5 billion of the world's population. The super-rich in a single country, the United States, have amassed $6.1 trillion.[158] Hence, on the one side we have a very few who would not be able to count their money in a lifetime at the rate of a dollar per second, to whom another zero on their ledger means about the same thing as a twenty-fifth car would mean to a person who already owns two dozen. On the other hand, we are faced with billions of people struggling in the abyss of appalling poverty, starving to death in unspeakable agony.

Money has a natural tendency to accumulate. One does not have to be a thief in order to become rich, although not everyone can be equally fortunate. Like water that flows into lakes and eventually into the sea, money has a way of accumulating under the influence of an attraction that is almost gravitational. It is the lifeblood of the economy—like water, again, we cannot do without it. If there were not a mechanism in nature, evaporation and precipitation, that redistributes water across the land mass, life could not long survive on this planet except in the seas. The lakes and seas are not perceptibly diminished by evaporation, and in any case it comes back to them sooner or later. But meanwhile, life is facilitated by this cycle; billions of creatures are enabled to live out their lives.

But we do not have the equivalent of the water cycle in

human affairs. So it has to be instituted artificially—voluntarily, it goes without saying, for this cannot be forced. In Islam, the alms-tax decreed by the Divine Law is reserved for the poor alone. I say alms-tax not because it is collected by the government, but because it is given to the poor annually at a specific rate that is not less than, but can be above, 2.5 percent of one's savings. "The alms-tax is enough for the poor if properly observed," remarked the Prophet. "If it hadn't been, God would have decreed additional means for their livelihood."

Just how right this observation is can be gleaned from the fact that according to estimates by the United Nations, the additional cost of achieving and maintaining universal access to basic education for all, basic health care for all, reproductive health care for all women, *adequate food* for all, and safe water and sanitation for all is roughly $40 billion a year. The UN explains: "This is less than 4 percent of the combined wealth of the richest 225 people."[159] Two and a half percent of the wealth of the world's richer half, donated annually to the poorer half, would in short order put an end to poverty on Earth without appreciably taxing the donors' means. This would have the effect not only of alleviating world poverty, but of preserving open society against the "capitalist threat," as Soros observes.

Note that the whole world doesn't have to embrace Islamic Sufism in order to do this. In the past, people have benefited from the applications of Sufi principles without themselves becoming Sufis. This is because those principles stand in linear superposition, and every little bit helps. (This is not to deny the synergy obtained when the principles are working in joint action.) Traditionally, Moslems have observed the alms-tax donation because it is part of their faith. But today, if observed universally, it promises the hope of a world freed of hunger and poverty, of strife and despair. The reason is that the economic and technological infrastructure painstakingly built up by man throughout the centuries has grown to such proportions that even misers can now afford to be benevolent. Today we possess true global wealth. And the world can become a veritable paradise if we choose to act self-lessly, humanely, altruistically, with only a small fraction of our earnings.

In this connection, even the food products destroyed in order to maintain prices could be given away to curb world hunger. In 1999, for example, the European Union donated a sum of DM 1 billion (ca. $533 million) for the destruction of fruit and vegetables.[160] We may be rich, but we're not *that* rich—no amount of wealth can survive that kind of squandering. Not only is this economically wasteful (the primary meaning of "economy" being the thrifty management or use of resources), it is also irrational in ecological terms, since the resources subject to destruction are near the top of the food pyramid. Instead of donating DM 1 billion to destroy food, why not donate the food itself, why not spend a fraction of that sum for its transportation and distribution to world regions stricken by hunger?

Incomprehensible. Simply incomprehensible.

•—•—•

This chapter examined the nature of society in the light of Islamic Sufism, which provides a holistic epistemology for uniting material and spiritual knowledge. It was emphasized that Islam favors no particular ideology, and that a society enlightened by Islamic Sufism is composed of people with a democratic personality structure. We suggested that the alms-tax can be used as a contemporary method to provide a speedy resolution to world poverty. Chapter 8 now describes the culmination of man's spiritual quest: the station beyond all stations.

8

THE STATION BEYOND ALL STATIONS

The name and sign of the sage do not appear
'Tis not wisdom to be "the son of such-and-such"
Who leaves his place has no space[161]
The People of Truth possess no signs.

They leave no trace that they should be known by their trace
They raise no dust that they should be known by their dust
Do not think they can be known by their words
The People of Truth possess no signs.

—NIYAZI MISRI

The Sufi Saint

Man is unresolved, he is unfinished. God has created him with the potential and the need to go beyond himself. To go beyond man means to fulfill what remains unfulfilled; it means to become more fully human in the best sense of the word, not less. More intelligent. More considerate. More loving. More helpful. Kinder. Abler. More awake. More conscious. More relaxed, yet more energetic.

To be more fully human, one has to go through all the experiences lived by ordinary human beings: childhood, education, work, marriage, having children and grandchildren. There are some Sufi orders that do advise withdrawal from the world, but by and large the goal of Sufism is to be approached through the thick of life, not by isolation or escapism. Seclusion is okay, but in the right dose, in the proper proportion, at the right time.

Our traditions have misinformed us about what it means to be a prophet, saint, or mystic. A prophet or sage is an ambassador to humanity. This means not just that such a person is an envoy, a messenger, of God—or the inheritor of an envoy—before humanity. It also means that he represents humanity to the divine. Such a person is a bridge on which the divine and the human meet—a truly universal point of fusion.

The Nature of the Encounter

Nothing you have ever seen, learned, or experienced has prepared you for your experience with a Perfect Human Being, assuming you ever meet one like the Master (which is a rare gift indeed). You may be the most sophisticated person, worldly-wise, seasoned. You may have scaled mountains, whether physically or intellectually or both. After all this is said and done, you will find yourself still totally unprepared for an encounter of that order.

What strikes you is that the various elements of the human personality—whatever these may be—are exactly balanced, in just the right amount and proportion relative to each other. There is nothing that sticks out, nothing that strikes a discordant note. Equally, you intuitively realize that this person is totally authentic. There is nothing fake about him. Not only that, but it is inconceivable that there even *could* be anything fake about him. That is the impression he leaves. When Walt Whitman wrote, "I and mine do not convince by arguments; we convince by our presence," he must have been talking about the Master. In view of such an example, human psychology has to be rewritten. The whole gamut of human possibilities has to be recast in a new light. Everything about such a human being is exceptional, yet his very existence is proof that such things are humanly possible. Had I not had the good fortune to see such a person (cf. the Prologue), I too would have had to remain content with our better-known versions of psychology. One such encounter is enough to tell you that all the famous names in psychology's hall of fame have missed not just something, but many things—so many, in fact, that we might as well wipe the slate clean and start afresh. (Of course, to give credit where it's due, this is not to deny the good many things they've got right. But a re-visioning is still called for.)

Naturally, you arrive at these conclusions only after long reflection, when you are able to view the event with hindsight and from a distance. The immediate experience of the encounter is overwhelming, assuming you're at all perceptive.

Having seen and heard things that nothing in our ordinary, secular world had prepared me for, I realize today that we live in Flatland. Because we have construed the world as a Hollywood prop, we have convinced ourselves that this is all there is to it. We have taken the world at face value, not looking for what is *signified* by these "signs." And the world has obliged us by appearing to be that way. But if we look closely enough, we will notice telltale discrepancies that eventually lead us out of the Labyrinth. Furthermore, we have been conned into thinking that this is all there is to *us*—and whatever else there is, *if* there is, is supposed to be vile and filthy.

At a certain point, I discovered that I had been laboring under three assumptions, none of which turned out to be true. I mention them here because they seem to be common in our age.

1. The assumption that religion is nothing but "the opium of the people."
2. The assumption that the beginning and end of the universe are too remote for eschatological considerations to have any bearing on everyday life.
3. The assumption of agnosticism: that nothing can be known about God, not even the question of whether He exists.

I was to see these three assumptions demolished one by one.

It was only by the greatest effort that I was able to find the Master, to gain admittance to the stronghold of Sufism, its very heartland, yet even then it was the grace of God and not my struggles that got me there.

What I found in the Master's teachings, and in his alone, was an *astonishing internal consistency*. What appeared, either in Islam or other religions/traditions, to be illogical or irrational would be explained in a way that made eminent sense. A datum or factotum might be given a slight twist, thanks to which a whole issue would be cast in an entirely new light. This, I became convinced, must be the "hidden wisdom" or "lost wisdom" we've heard so much about, carried on for posterity and into the twenty-first century through the famous Oral Tradition of the Sufis. It was as Claude Shannon theorized: the communication of information inevitably entails noise and the loss of part of that information. Only via a noise-free medium or zero-loss channel could the transmission of wisdom to future generations be ensured.

Just as Bernard Shaw said of the Prophet, the Master would solve the most difficult problems with the ease of sipping a cup of coffee. (In his case, it was a cup of tea.) His eyes would take on a distant look, or he would focus on something nearby, and when he pronounced on some issue, it would almost invariably

be the correct solution, borne out by subsequent events. I quali-
fy the preceding statement with "almost" because there might
have been exceptions of which I am unaware, but for all practical purposes that "almost" can be omitted.

Arthur C. Clarke once formulated what has become known
as Clarke's Law: "Any sufficiently advanced technology is indistinguishable from magic." In like manner, one could conjecture
that any sufficiently developed intelligence is indistinguishable
from the superhuman. Where does intelligence end? Where do
paranormal abilities begin? If we are merely draft copies of a
properly crystallized human being, what is it like to experience
that clarity?

The answer is that we cannot know, in the same way that the
darkness cannot comprehend the light that shines therein. But we
can try to understand, to gain some inkling, however faint, of
what it must be like. For, *in potentia,* that light is within us all.
It is outside the reach of none, but no one is aware of it. Since
the Master has now departed, it remains for me, unequal to the
task as I am, to unravel the essence of his teachings and of
Turkish Sufism for posterity.

Awakening

In the following sayings of the Prophet and verses of the Book
is contained the possibility of another mode of being:

"People are asleep; they wake up when they die."
"Die before you die."
"Who dies once, does not die again."
"Every self shall taste of death" (3:185, 29:57).
"We do not die, except for our first death"
     (37:58-59, also 44:56).

These lines herald the possibility of a breakthrough for man: the possibility of Sufi sainthood ("the Friendship of God"). For, in addition to the general topography of the after-death state (heaven, hell, etc.), we are being informed of a state where a human being can awaken *before physical death*. And this awakening is of such a nature that immortality is realized, for waking up also means waking up to the realization that you are immortal: "Even if you are buried, there will be no corpse in your coffin" (Gustav Meyrink).

This is metaphorical, of course (for Sufis, too, physically die). It means that one will have joined the Immortals and be free of the heaven/hell dilemma that is our usual fare in the after-death state. It means that one becomes Enlightened, inundated by divine light, and achieves a state difficult to comprehend or describe in ordinary terms. For just as heaven is "above" (superior to, etc.) hell, there is a condition that is "above" heaven, and the truly intelligent do not care a fig for heaven in view of that higher prospect. There is a narrow path that leads through the "crack between the opposites"—between white and black, being and nonbeing, heaven and hell, etc.—to this other state. Because it is beyond all multiplicity, we can call it Unity (*wahdah*); the path itself we can call Unification (*tawhid*).

Spiritual Embryogenesis

To "die before you die" is to be born again, to experience spiritual rebirth. Hence, one who has "awakened"—in the present sense of the term—is twice-born.

Throughout history, the deepest and most profound core of all esoteric teachings has been reserved for the "child of the spirit." In Sufism it is called the Child of Meaning (*tifl al-maani*) or Child of the Heart (*walad al-qalb*). In Hinduism, its name is the

Golden Germ or Golden Child (*hiranya-garbha*). In Alchemy it is the *homunculus,* symbolically masked by being born in a retort. In Chinese Taoism it is the "immortal foetus," "embryo of the Tao," "seed pearl" or "starseed embryo." In ancient Egypt it is the spirit-child Horus, son of Osiris. In Roman antiquity it is the "eternal boy" or "eternal youth" (*puer aeternus*). In Buddhism it is the "son of the Buddha."[162] Wonder of wonders, it has sprouted spontaneously even out of atheistic soil. Just as Nietzsche was able to conceive of the Superman, Stanley Kubrick and Arthur Clarke were able to conceive the Star-Child in their science-fiction movie/novel *2001: A Space Odyssey.*

Traditionally, it is fertilized and nurtured in the (spiritual) Heart. The retort in which the *homunculus* gestates is a symbol for the Heart. Moreover, the child grows. It passes through childhood and youth. The Son of the Buddha grows up to inherit the Diamond Body of the Buddha. The Star-Child grows up to become the Superman. The Child of the Heart Ascends to become the Perfect Human.

In his Commentary on *The Secret of the Golden Flower,* Carl G. Jung called Eastern philosophers "symbolical psychologists, to whom no greater wrong could be done than to take them literally."[163] I must insist, however, that whatever additional meanings we may glean from a symbolic interpretation, the child of the spirit is meant, by all parties in the know, in a literal sense. Much in the philosophy of the East is metaphorical, but not always.

The great Sufi Sage Abdulqader Geylani says the following about the Child of the Heart:

> This name is given to it metaphorically, because it is concerned with the body and has assumed human form. It is the truth of humanity. Since it has nothing to do with matter, its existence does not constitute a veil to the Essence of

God. A Tradition expresses this as follows: "I have a time with God such that no angel close to God and no Prophet can come between us." The "Prophet" in this saying includes the human aspect of the Prophet of God.

In another Tradition, our Prophet has stated: "I saw my Lord in the form of a beautiful youth (*shaab al-amrad*)."

This is *the child of the heart*. It is God's manifestation in that form.

What the possessor of knowledge needs to understand is this truth of humanity called the child of meaning. He needs to pass beyond the corporeal world to the spiritual world—the Secret World. Nothing exists there except the Essence of God. This is an infinite expanse where the child of meaning takes flight. There it sees strange and wonderful things, but it is impossible to convey information about them to others. This is the station of the People of Unity, who have found extinction (*fana*) from their own existence.

Jesus has said: "Unless a man is born again, he cannot enter the Kingdom of God."[164]

Birds, too, are twice-born. In its first birth, the bird consists of an egg. If it is not reborn, leaving its shell behind, it can never fly.

What is meant by this is birth in the world of meaning, the spiritual world. This latent capacity in man is the secret of humanity. It is realized by the combination of the sciences of Divine Law and Gnosis, just as the union of "two waters" forms a child.[165]

Elsewhere he adds, in a similar context: "Do not ask for proofs. For these phenomena being described are beyond the book of reason."

But granted that there is such a thing as a spiritual child, and that it is a good idea to nurture it, how can this be done? Here I can only provide a hint by referring to a statement of the Master: "*Everything* is included in the Formal Prayer. *Everything.*" (His emphasis.) To elaborate a bit, the Heart-Child is in the Formal Prayer, the Ascension (*meeraj*) is in the Formal Prayer, The Perfect Human is in the Formal Prayer—if only it is properly performed.

The process by which the spirit-child matures is accompanied by great effort (*mujahada*). This struggle involves abstraction (*tajarrud*), isolating one's self from everything. The self has to be stripped of all human attributes in order to remain clothed in divine attributes. To achieve this, one has to love God more than one loves oneself. As the Turkish Sufi poet Yunus Emre elaborates:

Your love has removed me from myself
It's you I need, and you alone.
By day and by night I burn
It's you I need, and you alone.

What they pine for: "Heaven, Heaven"
Is but a few villas, a few houris.[166]
Give them to whoever wants them
It's you I need, and you alone.

The fiery poet of divine love, Rumi, sums it up: "I was raw, I was cooked, I burned," to which Yunus adds: "My fire increases each passing day." "Slay me with your love," sings he. "Your love slays lovers, it immerses them in the sea of love." He also speaks of the intoxicating "wine of love," and indeed, wine is a stock item in Sufi literature as a symbol for divine love.

A drop of its fire makes oceans boil
I fell into the fire of love, I ignited and I burned

This is purification by fire, for one's human attributes are burned away by that all-consuming fire. The legendary beast, the phoenix, is consumed in its own fire, and out of its ashes steps the new phoenix, the spirit-child.

Poverty and Self-emptying

The concept of *faqr* in Sufism denotes spiritual poverty. It stands for purifying the self of everything-other-than-God (*masi-wa*), and concentrating the attention on God alone. One must make oneself transparent to God. By shedding one's animal and all-too-human attributes, by removing those layers, one allows divine attributes to shine through. "One should pass," says the Grand Sheikh Abdulqader Geylani, "from poverty [P] to poverty from poverty [P^2], and then to poverty from poverty from poverty [P^3]." It is thus that one reaches the Station of No Station. He continues: "When poverty is completed in this way, the result is God. The (spiritually) poor is not a person in need, but someone whose every word comes true." Or, as a Turkish Sufi expression has it,

> You get out from in between,
> And the Creator at once is seen.

But who sees the Creator? Is it you or me? The Prophet said, "God is a Light. How can I see Him?" No. According to another Sufi saying, "It is through Himself that God is known." In other words, when no one and nothing remains other than God, then He is clearly perceived. Herein lies the basic fallacy of those who ask proofs of God: as long as you can distinguish anything other than God, you cannot perceive God. As one mystic put it: "He who sees not God everywhere, sees Him truly nowhere." Cognition of

Multiplicity and cognition of Unity do not mix. Thus we have two distinct frames of reference: the former belongs to existence in general, the latter is the God's-eye point of view. All that we witness in this world is a "sign," a pointer to Him. Thus we do not see Him (as He sees Himself) *essentially;* we see the variety of His attributes and through them we come to know Unity.

He who tastes of Unity
Is liberated from duality.

The Sufis have compared Multiplicity (*kasrah*) to waves on the ocean; Unity (*wahdah*) to the ocean itself. The waves are, of course, not separate from the ocean. Yet the ocean is not the waves, and because, in ordinary life, we concentrate so much on waves, we cannot see the ocean for the waves.

Becoming God-transparent is realized by purifying the (spiritual) Heart. God states in a Holy Tradition: "The heavens and the earth do not contain me, yet the Heart of my believing servant does." The Heart is actually the Throne of God; it is the window through which God's light (divine *lux/an-nur*, not physical *lumen/az-ziya*) shines upon the universe. But our hearts have become clouded over with troubles, worries, attachments, and cravings. They have become encrusted with spiritual cobwebs and dirt. When we clean that window, Presto!—God's light will shine through it again. In the words of the Sufi poet Sham'i:

Nobody attains the Truth until one is distant from all
The treasure is not revealed to a Heart until it is full of light

Drive out all else from the Heart till the Real is manifest
The king does not enter the palace till it is magnificent

So, a human being must strive to attain self-effacement. This is how he is to overcome himself, to finish the process that God started in creating us. The equivalent of this in the New Testament is called *kenosis* (after Philippians 2:7), "self-emptying." When this process is finished, the result is *fana fi-Allah,* "extinction in God." Now the Sufi concept of *fana* (extinction, annihilation) has its direct correlate in Buddhism: *Nirvana,* which means extinguishing (literally, the snuffing out of a candle).

We thus see that this process of *faqr* leading to *fana fi-Allah* in Sufism brings together four great religions: Islam, Christianity, Buddhism, and Hinduism. For Islam is already implicit in Sufism. "Blessed are the poor in spirit, for theirs is the kingdom of heaven" (Matthew 5:3) and "Blessed are the pure in heart, for they shall see God" (Matthew 5:8) is the way Jesus sermonized it on the Mount. And the formula *fana fi-Allah* means "Nirvana in Brahman" in terms of Buddhism and Hinduism, thus unexpectedly uniting, at a single stroke, these two great yet apparently disparate traditions. And the term *sunnah-Allah,* the "way" or "custom" of God, introduces *Tao,* "the Way." (Also God, if *Tao* is taken in the sense of "meaning.")

(In fact, it may be a latent truth of comparative religion that when a single religious path is not sufficient to meet the diverse needs of people in a culture, two or three coexist, complementing each other. In Western culture, Judaism is inclined more towards the exoteric, Christianity towards the esoteric. In India, Hinduism indicates the goal, Buddhism the path. In China, Confucianism is about form and conduct, Taoism about content and mysticism. A path that is all-inclusive would fulfill all needs and hence obviate the need for any other path.)

The Paint of God

The journey to God cannot be accomplished in one step. This is why it is a long, drawn-out process composed of intermediate steps. The Sufis have many ways of talking about these steps, and one of them is that extinction in God is preceded by, first, extinction in one's master (*fana fish-sheikh*), and then extinction in the Prophet (*fana fir-rasul*). Extinction in God is capped by a further step, subsistence in God (*baqa bi-Allah*).

It is in the first of these that the seeker implores, "Lift away my self from me, Master" (Shamsi). All the while, one prays—with Yunus—to God, who is the true goal of the journey:

Remove me-ness from me, with you-ness fill me
Take my life while in this life[167]
Let me not die over there.

In Yunus' way of thinking, the goal is to bring out the wonderful inner self within man, the divine self of the Perfect Human:

Do not say I am in me, because I am not
There is an I inside me, inner than myself.

As we have already seen, the Sufis pass through various stages during their progress along the Path. This is comparable to peeling off the layers of an onion. As various layers of base attributes are burned away, one or another divine attribute manifests itself. It is as if one becomes "painted" in that attribute. Furthermore, there is a distinction between "states," which are only temporary, and "stations," which represent permanent gains. The Sufis have referred to this shifting situation as "variation" (*talwin*, lit. "coloring"). It is important, however, to leave this stage behind and to achieve "stability" (*tamqin*, "to settle down"), where all divine attributes become permanently manifest and fully balanced. If, after realization, a color remains—if an attribute or attributes can be distinguished—it is because "The color of water is the color of its container," in the words of Junayd of Baghdad.

It is the master's task to instruct the disciple, the disciple's responsibility to carry out those instructions. "The sages do but show the way."

At first, the disciple merely imitates the master. As the conduct and ways of the master gradually become ingrained in the disciple, realization becomes a possibility. This passage from imitation (*taqlid*) to realization (*tahqiq*) might be described as "fake it till you make it."

But what is realization like?

Consider white light. It is composed of light of all wavelengths, of red and blue and yellow and green, yet no color preponderates or stands out. In the same way, once all stations, each with a distinctive quality, have been left behind, one reaches a stage where all qualities are in full balance. Hence, this station is colorless. This is the color of God, and indeed Sufis have spoken of being painted with "the paint of God" (itself a Koranic term).

As Ibn Arabi said: "The people of perfection have realized all stations and states and passed beyond these to the station above both majesty and beauty, so they have no attribute and no description."[168] They are at once at every station and at none of them in particular. William Chittick, who provides this quotation from Arabi, further explains: "The Station of No Station brings together every opposite quality in utter undifferentiation, pure unity, sheer consciousness, total freedom, complete lack of delimitation, and identity with the Real's self-disclosures. The nature of the consciousness experienced in this station can only be expressed in analogies and metaphors. It is utterly inaccessible to ordinary language, which is to say that people are blind to the shining of its light. In fact, of course, the light witnessed by perfect human beings is forever shining in the darkness of the cosmos; it is only human incapacity that prevents people from seeing it."[169]

Sages cannot be known by their outward appearance. They

cannot be distinguished from other, ordinary people on this basis. It is only by his or her inner status that a sage can be recognized. But how to discern the inner world of another? Another Sufi saying comes to the rescue: "Whatever is in the (earthenware) jug oozes out." And the superfluid helium II climbs out and flows over the rim of its containment vessel (e.g. a Dewar flask), or through tiny holes impervious to any other liquid. In this respect, it is very much like the self. Similarly, the inner state of a person is reflected in that person's outward *behavior*. It is by the sublime conduct, the Godly manners, s/he exhibits that a sage is known.

Culmination

If one travels long enough on the footpath of the prophets, the saints, and the mystics, one arrives at length in the proximity of where they arrived. One arrives, in other words, at the limits of the universe. That is where the journey to God leads if one follows the Path faithfully enough. The next thing to do is to step out of the universe.

One does not reach that destination by travelling physically outward. Rather, it is reached in the realm of consciousness, by travelling to our inmost center.

This is the last station, the final stop. It is marked by the "Lote-tree of the Boundary" (*sidra al-muntaha*). Beyond it, the universe ends, and the Transfinite begins.

When the Prophet experienced his Ascension, the archangel Gabriel accompanied him as his guide. But when they arrived at the Boundary, Gabriel froze.

"I can go no further," he said. "If I take another step, I shall burn, for nothing finite can exist beyond this point."

The Prophet said, "If I must burn, by all means let me," and crossed the threshold without hesitation. He was consumed in the infinite love of God.

Unity, Infinity, Eternity engulfed him.

How can such a state be described?

Infinite bliss. Infinite consciousness. Infinite existence. Infinite love. Infinite light.

I say infinity, but this is beyond even the infinite, for mathematical infinity itself has a limit. Infinite series can converge to a limit, and in any case all infinities are confined to the realm of numbers.

This is an Infinite Unity, wondrous beyond all imagination. I shall not break with the tradition of all mystics by trying, in vain, to describe the indescribable. "Whoever attains the mystery of Unity—his tongue is sealed, his mind vanquished."

For beyond all stations is the Station of No Station, the Station of Praise (*maqam al-mahmud*), where the servant has humbly effaced himself to such a degree that the distance between his self and Reality has become as thin as an onion skin, a transparent film. That station belongs only to the Prophet, and those who have followed him closely enough have been able to arrive at a point not far distant.

The ultimate realization is that nothing exists *but* the Real. The universe and everything in it only have a comparative existence, while Absolute Being belongs to God alone. To quote Yunus again:

Dearest Lord, you said to me:
"I am closer to you than you."
If you are thus close to me
Show me your magnificent face.

How come you're close to me?
I miss you and long for you.
I watch for you day and night,
But can't see you and blame myself.

—and then he continues:

It is He who comes, He who goes
He is the seer, He the seen
Sublime and base, everything
The seen is He, so see Him!

Yunus, *this is the mystery of Truth*
This cannot be put into words
It is a taste (pleasure) to know this
Mind and conception can't attain to it.

Another Turkish Sufi poet, Harabi, has written:

Our words are, beyond doubt, the truth
Who is born, who dies, who makes, who destroys is the Truth
Wherever you look is Absolute Truth[170]
We have proclaimed the conditions of Unity.

And Yunus again:

Yunus Emre *disappeared*
All his being became Truth[171]
Besides Him there is nothing
I do not remain in doubt.

●━●━●

In this chapter we have described the ultimate state of the realized self, one that paradoxically possesses no "sign" of its own, since it fully comprises Meaning in the universe—self-purification leaving "the paint of God" exposed. The Formal Prayer is again identified as the locus for this sacred rebirth, leading to the ultimate realization that nothing exists but the Real.

At which point, one is issued the command to "Return" (*irjii*)—to the ordinary world, the sensory world, the world of human beings—in order to serve the prophetic and bodhisattvic ideal: to save as many as one can. Who was once a disciple himself becomes a master—but only after realization is achieved, not before: "Until the candle was kindled, it did not burn the moth."

To return in order to help others out of Plato's Cave,
Out of this comparative dungeon;
To help them from the darkness
    Into Light.

Appendix

FUNDAMENTALISM AND THE TALIBAN

In recent years, fundamentalism has increasingly come to dominate discussions on Islam. But fundamentalism is not what Islam is all about, and it is not what this book is all about.

However, the question needs to be addressed, if only because of the widespread interest in the topic. Of course, any detailed treatment of fundamentalism would have to constitute a separate book, such as Karen Armstrong's recent *The Battle for God* (2000) or John L. Esposito's *The Islamic Threat: Myth or Reality?* (1992). Nevertheless, I believe the subject can be addressed briefly by focusing on a specific example. While each case would have to be studied under its own circumstances, the phenomenon of the Taliban provides enough pointers to allow some general observations to be made.

The Taliban is basically a geopolitical repercussion of the Cold War. Ahmed Rashid, who has written an authoritative book on the Taliban, states that before the Afghan war, "the Islam traditionally practiced in Afghanistan was also immensely tolerant—of other Muslim sects, other religions and different lifestyles. . . . Traditional Islam in Afghanistan believed in minimum government with as little state interference as possible. Another key factor contributing to Afghan tolerance was the enormous popularity of Sufism, a mystical and undogmatic branch of Islam."[172]

But then came the Soviets. The first thing that sticks in my mind whenever I think about the Afghan war is that the Russians planted doll- and toy-shaped bombs (mines) for little children. They would pick these up, thinking to play with them. The bombs would explode at their feet, in their hands, or near their faces. Many were killed or maimed for life. Yes, that's how the Russians waged the war. Tacitus wrote that the Roman army left a wasteland in its wake and called it peace, and the same holds for the Russians, only more so. When they finally left, the fragile tissue that held a nation together had been destroyed. The region had become permanently destabilized. Factions that had earlier fought together against the enemy now fought against each other to gain control of the country, but to no avail. And anyone who knows anything about civil war also knows that it is the only thing that can be worse than war itself. It was out of this kind of environment that the Taliban was spawned.

A simple experiment in biology demonstrates what happened next: place a certain white flower in clean water. It will remain white. Spike the water with red ink, and after a while the colored water traveling up to the petals of the flower will turn it pink. The blood that lay at the roots of the Taliban ensured that its leaves would be long on wrath and short on bliss, with all the tolerance and kindness washed out by the war and subsequent civil war. It is the offshoot of a people driven against the wall—ravaged by war, living in socioeconomic conditions of utter destitution, and lacking all means of education other than the traditional rote memorization of the Koran. In a land where nothing is right, it's not as if Islam according to the Taliban is the only thing that's distorted.

This is not meant to justify the actions of the Taliban, but to help us understand how it came about and why it is an exceptional case. Which is also why it attracts so much media attention: "man bites dog" is news precisely because it is so unusual, whereas the vast majority of Moslems peacefully going about their affairs every day never receive a mention.

If the reports in the Western media emerging from Afghanistan are anything to go by, the Talibanic brand of Islam practiced there leaves much to be desired.[173] The mutual mistrust and incomprehension only serve to perpetuate a dialogue of the deaf.

We seem to be beset with Islamophobia, and wherever there is a deep-seated, irrational fear, it is sure to drive out rational cogitation. We seem to regard Islam as an alien threat, expecting a religious revolution and a worldwide Holy War to spread like wildfire any moment. This is not going to happen, for the simple reason that Islam has many faces. It is not an implacable, monolithic bloc. Nor is Central Asia about to be "taken over" by a handful of Taliban. The Talibanization that *did* occur in Pakistan is the result of its own actions. Because it wished to control the affairs of its neighbor through the Taliban, but possessed almost the same ethnic and social fabric as Afghanistan, it was not immune to the forces it would itself unleash. So it is unreasonable to expect that Talibanization will spread further, along the lines of a "Domino theory" earlier applied to communism. The region today is ruled by what experts characterize as a "criminalized war economy," heavily dependent for its financing on drug traffic. As Rashid has pointed out elsewhere, "The Taliban needs hard cash to maintain its army. Unlike the volunteers that fought the former Soviet Union, many Taliban soldiers are paid mercenaries." Which also shows that it is unpopular with the masses. And Pakistan has paid heavily for this, with practically zero drug addicts in 1980 and three to five million addicts in the 1990s. Maya Chadda observed that "Pakistan's Taliban strategy for regional influence had boomeranged."[174] Further, as Peter

Tomsen remarks, the semiliterate Taliban's authoritarianism and intolerance have alienated the Afghans themselves, a prelude to its eventual disintegration.[175]

Speaking of Pakistan, weapons of mass destruction are a universal evil, which the Master always spoke—and in fact prepared pamphlets—against. The fact that Pakistan is an "Islamic" country does not make the atomic bombs in its possession any less evil. Unless these Doomsday weapons are banned immediately, unequivocally, and universally, they will sooner or later spell the end of humankind, a fact that those in authority ignore at our common peril.

And here is another note for policy-makers: if you fear an outbreak of malaria, the solution is not to hunt down individual mosquitos and shoot them in the eye. The wise thing to do is to transform the marshland into a verdant pasture. Rehabilitate Afghan society, heal its wounds, for your own good and for the good of the world. (One need only remember the Marshall Plan here.) Is this so difficult to accomplish on Earth, when we can already think of making a whole planet—Mars—habitable through "planetary engineering"?

But most of all, it seems amazing that after so many centuries, we still do not know enough about Islam. It is a truism that one always fears the unknown. Before I became acquainted with the Sufis, a stereotype invented by a derisive left-wing cartoonist colored my views about followers of Sufi orders: barbaric, club-wielding, black-bearded bigots. Nothing could be further from the truth. In the quarter-century that I have known Sufis, I have come across only one person who even remotely resembled this stereotype—a harmless old codger with a white beard—and the resemblance was in appearance only, not in character. Now the same holds for Islam—matters are greatly eased, and it's a tremendous relief, when you realize that Moslems are just ordinary folks like you and me. At long last, we have to wake up and recognize that the God who sent down Revelation to Mohammed is the same God who saved Noah from the Flood, the same God who spoke to Moses on the mountain, and the same God who sent Jesus forth to spread the message of brotherly love. In that recognition lies our mutual salvation.

As for the Taliban and similar movements: their actions, says Michael Jansen, "show Muslims—and by implication their religion—to be intolerant, harsh and bloodthirsty. Unfortunately, these actions speak louder than the words of God set down in the Koran 14 centuries ago, louder than the just pronouncements of the Prophet Muhammad, louder than the voices of learned jurists who, over the centuries, developed a body of law and practice (the 'Sharia') far more enlightened for their time than that in Europe. These examples are not of mainstream Muslim behaviour, expressive of the writ and spirit of Islam or indicative of the teachings of the Prophet. These are examples drawn from the behaviour patterns of tribesmen come to town. Behaviour patterns, indeed, which are pre-Islamic and have little to do with the code of conduct laid down in the Koran and the 'traditions' or 'hadith' of the Prophet.

". . . The Taliban is a movement of militant Sunni Muslim Afghan tribesmen from the south of the country. Rural people who live hard lives and employ harsh sanctions to ensure a modicum of order within their closely circumscribed world."[176]

Ignorance is the root of all evil. In his preface to *Androcles and the Lion*, Bernard Shaw wrote: "[W]hen the religion of the high mind is offered to the lower mind, the lower mind, feeling its fascination without understanding it, and being incapable of rising to it, drags it down to its level by degrading it. Years ago I said that the conversion of a savage to Christianity is the conversion of Christianity to savagery." It is my observation, after many years of close study and thinking, that Islamic movements which base themselves exclusively on the Koran, without the temperance of and the lofty ethical precedent set by the Prophet and the greatest of his followers, invariably lack a crucial ingredient, a hermeneutic if you wish, that restores beauty and spirit to the letter of the Holy Law—the latter remains solely legalistic under such circumstances. Whereas religion—any religion—is always something more than a legal code, just as a human being is more than a skeleton, and the Koran itself indicates explicitly that the Prophet's example should be followed. All forms of extremism go against the leniency, moderation, and restraint (even in war) of the Prophet. They represent a form of Islam cut off from its spiritual wellsprings.

The Koran and the Prophet's Radiant Way have always been the two pillars of Islam. We would be making a grave mistake were we to emphasize the former at the expense of the latter. For in paying attention to the "Silent Koran," i.e., the Book, we run the risk of ignoring the "Speaking Koran," i.e., the Prophet himself. The Koran is an absolute text: the fact that it can be translated should not lead to the superficial perception that it can be easily understood. On the contrary, it is like the human genome—quite abstruse and incomprehensible in many respects. That is why its translation into human form is needed—without the Model of the Prophet to go by, Moslems would fall astray in the most elementary things. And in each age, there have been faithful followers who have emulated that exemplar with precision. Such people interpret the Koran for the understanding of us all.

Having seen, in the person of the Master, what *real* Islam is like, I hope you will forgive me if I take great exception to all forms of "fundamentalism." He was the living embodiment of the Prophet's teachings: the closest human being to that Model in our day and age, in the grand tradition of all earlier prophets and saints. On the basis of that example, I can clearly state that fundamentalism is not the spirit of Islam, however much it may selectively adhere to the letter of the Sharia. Fanaticism and terrorism run directly counter to the universal love radiated by the Master and the Prophet himself. His was a crystallization of, and not merely a topsy-turvy selection from, both the Book and the Way of the Prophet. In the face of that synthesis, all other interpretations must pale into insignificance. As for the concept of *jihad,* which is usually translated as Holy War, this term actually means "struggle" in the way of God—with our possessions and our selves. While the Prophet did wage war, he opted for peace whenever possible, and on returning from one battle, declared: "We now go from the lesser war to the greatest war." He explained that this greatest war meant struggle with our selves, struggle against the Base Self.

This is why the Book and the Prophetic example *in combination* must always be the reference point. These, and not the Taliban or any self-appointed authority claiming to speak in their name, must inspire the beliefs and actions of Moslems. And in order to facilitate this, we must all—Moslems and non-Moslems alike—disabuse ourselves of our ignorance.

Now it may be true that the Taliban, being tribal, took the religion of Islam and tribalized it. But we must also remember that Islam first emerged in a tribal society, civilized it, and paved the way for one of the world's great civilizations. If the Taliban are now tribalizing Islam, their influence—no matter what the intentions behind it—is diametrically opposite. However strenuously they may protest the purity of their faith, the acid test comes when we realize that people looked at the Prophet, his Companions, and their followers and concluded (even when they were not converted): "I like this religion. There are things in it that appeal to me." In this day and age, it is incumbent on all

Moslems to beware of leading people to the reverse conclusion—
"I want no part of this religion"—to beware of bringing shame
and defamation upon Islam, a discredit it does not deserve. One
will not ingratiate oneself with God and His Prophet, nor achieve
one's goals, whatever these may be, by giving Islam a bad name.

ENDNOTES

PREFACE

1. Born in Eastern Anatolia, the enigmatic George I. Gurdjieff traveled widely in Asia in search of secret wisdom. In his communications to the West, he relied heavily on Sufi lore. Gurdjieff cannot be pinned down to any single tradition, because he made liberal and eclectic use of far too diverse traditions, perhaps even inventing some of his material along the way. In so doing, he lifted huge chunks of Sufi wisdom and transported them unchanged to a Western setting even while leaving out many essential things, as anyone with sufficient knowledge of Sufism will recognize when studying the Gurdjieff literature.

2. Hans Koning, "Notes on the Twentieth Century," *The Atlantic Monthly,* September 1997, pp. 90–100.

3. Robert D. Kaplan, "The Coming Anarchy," *The Atlantic Monthly,* February 1994, pp. 44–76.

PROLOGUE

4. In *The Philosophy of Physical Science* (1958), physicist Arthur Eddington compared the scientist to an ichthyologist who draws fish of a certain size out of the sea using a net with a cer-

tain mesh size, and then claims that *all* fish in the sea can only be this size.

5. This is based on Schliemann's own account, as related in C.W. Ceram's (Kurt W. Marek) *Gods, Graves and Scholars.* I take note that subsequent research seems to have cast doubt on certain aspects of his account.

6. J.L. Borges, "The Mirror of Enigmas" (tr. James E. Irby), *Labyrinths,* Harmondsworth, England: Penguin, 1970, pp. 244–47.

7. J.L. Borges, "The Approach to al-Mu'tasim" (tr. Anthony Kerrigan), *Ficciones,* New York: Grove Press, 1962, pp. 37–43. The following lines are also inspired by this story, and are based on it. What is interesting is that in large measure it corresponds to the truth, which is why I could find no better source of inspiration.

8. "Ahmet Kayhan Efendi," *Akit,* September 16, 1998.

INTRODUCTION

9. Alain Touraine, *Critique of Modernity,* (tr. David Macey), Oxford: Blackwell, 1995 [1992], p. 187.

10. Not a bad thing in itself from the Sufi point of view.

1. NIETZSCHE, GOD, AND DOOMSDAY: THE CONSEQUENCES OF ATHEISM

11. The original essay that forms the basis for this chapter is slated for publication in: Weaver Santaniello (ed.), *Nietzsche and the Gods,* New York: State University of New York Press, 2001.

12. Paraphrase from longer quotation in Nasr, *Man and Nature*, Kuala Lumpur: Foundation for Traditional Studies, 1986 [1968], p. 20.

13. Goethe, *Faust II*, verses 6227, 6246–48.

14. Quoted in Erich Heller, *The Importance of Nietzsche*, Chicago: University of Chicago Press, 1988, p. 5.

15. Ibid.

16. "Gott ist tot" rhymes in German, presumably with its own peculiar reverberations in Nietzsche's psyche.

17. Friedrich Nietzsche, *The Gay Science* (referred to below as *GS*), Walter Kaufmann (tr.), New York: Vintage Books, 1974 [1882, 1887]. (The "gay [or joyous] science" is actually poetry, which Emerson, esteemed by Nietzsche, claimed to be a professor of.)

18. *GS*, pp. 181–82.

19. Ibid. p. 279n3.

20. R.J. Hollingdale, *A Nietzsche Reader*, Harmondsworth, England: Penguin, 1977, p. 187.

21. Heller, p. 130.

22. In *Human, All Too Human*, Nietzsche outlines some of his objections to the Christian God: "A god who begets children on a mortal woman; a sage who calls upon us no longer to work . . .; a justice which accepts an innocent man as a substitute sacrifice; someone who bids his disciples drink his blood; . . . sins perpetrated against a god atoned for by [the same] god; . . . the figure

of the Cross as a symbol in an age which no longer knows the meaning and shame of the cross. . . ." (Quoted in Hollingdale, pp. 168–69.)

23. Quoted in Heller, p. 11.

24. See C.G. Jung, *Nietzsche's Zarathustra* (Notes of a seminar given in 1934–39), 2 vols. James L. Jarrett (ed.), Princeton: Princeton University Press (Bollingen Series), 1988, vol. 2, p. 1374.

25. *The Antichrist,* Section 16, in Walter Kaufmann (ed.), *The Portable Nietzsche,* New York: Viking Press, 1968 [1954] (referred to below as *VPN*), p. 582.

26. Ibid., Section 55, p. 642.

27. *GS,* Section 344, p. 281.

28. Polanyi, *Science, Faith and Society,* Chicago: University of Chicago Press, 1964 [1946], p. 45.

29. Polanyi, *Scientific Thought and Social Reality,* New York: International University Press, 1974, p. 51.

30. *GS,* Section 344, pp. 281–82.

31. Heller, p. 8.

32. *GS,* Section 345, pp. 282–83.

33. E.A. Burtt, *The Metaphysical Foundations of Modern Science,* New York: Doubleday Anchor, 1955.

34. *GS,* Section 345, p. 283.

35. Ibid.

36. Ibid. Section 109, p. 168.

37. Jacques Barzun, "Science versus Theology," in J.A. Garraty and Peter Gay (eds.), *The Columbia History of the World,* New York: Columbia University Press, 1972, p. 719.

38. Quoted in Leslie Paul Thiele, *Friedrich Nietzsche and the Politics of the Soul,* Princeton, N.J.: Princeton University Press, 1990, p. 108 (*Will to Power* 335).

39. Ibid. p. 109 (*Twilight of the Idols* 38, *Human, All Too Human* 323, *GS* 300).

40. Quoted in Laurence Lampert, *Nietzsche's Teaching,* New Haven: Yale University Press, 1986, p. 298 (*Will to Power* 1).

41. Here, time is linear. In *Zarathustra* he introduces the concept of circular time.

42. See Jung, vol. 2, pp. 1341–42. Nietzsche would have been familiar with the cosmic cycle constituted by the Greek mythological sequence of the Four Ages (Gold, Silver, Bronze, Iron) which in turn has its counterpart in the Hindu Round of the Four Yugas, after which the cycle repeats itself. Note the similarity with the four seasons in a year.

43. *GS*, Section 109, p. 168.

44. "God is dead; God died of his pity for man." (The devil, to Zarathustra, in *VPN*, p. 202. Also related: the godless Pope, "pity choked/strangled him," pp. 372–3.) The insights that God here refers to Christ, and that the Crucifixion is the act of supreme pity, belong to Professor Jung (Jung, pp. 997–98).

45. *The Antichrist,* Section 47, in *VPN,* p. 627; translation of the Latin formula given in footnote. This equation of God with a human being was not dominant initially, but proceeded step by step, culminating with the Council of Nicaea in 324 A.D., where Ossius (or Hosius), a follower of Athanasius, caused Emperor Constantine to declare and impose upon the bishops the formula: *homo-ousios* ("of the same essence"). But its seeds were already present in Paul's epistles.

46. Hollingdale, p. 212.

47. There is one sense in which Nietzsche's concept of *Beyond Good and Evil* is justified. God is Absolute Unity, i.e., beyond all multiplicity and duality. Hence in approaching God, passing beyond dualities and opposites would be a valid project—if Nietzsche believed in God. But even then, God can only be approached from the side of the good, for this is how He, who is beyond all need, desires it for us. The reason is that in psychic/spiritual/inner space, good is up and evil is down, with God at the zenith or summit. To disregard good and evil disorientates man, so it becomes terribly easy for him to land in the domain of absolute evil, in the abyss of Hell. For Nietzsche with his Protestant background, however, "beyond good and evil" paradoxically implies Paradise, the blissful state prior to the Fall of Man, before he ate the fruit of "the tree of knowledge of good and evil."

48. Ahmed Sirhindi (Imam Rabbani), *Mektubat* ("Letters," Ar.-Turk. tr. Kasim Yayla), Istanbul: Merve, 1999, vol. 1, p. 150 (52nd Letter).

49. In 1884, Nietzsche quotes Plato: "Each of us would like to be master, if possible, over all men, and best of all, God"—to which Nietzsche adds: "This attitude must exist again" (quoted in Lampert, p. 326n10: Plato *Theages* 126a, *Will to Power* 958).

50. *Gesammelte Werke* 14:43, quoted in Thiele, p. 193.

51. J.P. Stern, *A Study of Nietzsche,* Cambridge: Cambridge University Press, 1979, p. 31.

52. Jung, p. 903 (6 May 1936).

53. Hollingdale, p. 239. I have preferred "suspended" to Hollingdale's "fastened."

54. Ibid. p. 245.

55. Thiele, p. 66 (*Human, All Too Human* 197).

56. Hollingdale, p. 246.

57. Ibid. p. 247. It is actually not correct to state that the higher man is accidental, for this type can only be realized by the Great Work, and needs the utmost cultivation.

58. Ibid. p. 248.

59. Jung, vol. 2, p. 792.

60. The seven devils can also be interpreted as the seven deadly sins. In Sufism, the devil's deceits are ineffectual after Stage Four. See Chapter 4.

61. Hollingdale, p. 244.

62. *Twilight of the Idols,* Section 35, in *VPN,* pp. 535–36.

63. Hollingdale, p. 247. "Zarathustra the godless" also prefigures all our latter-day would-be gurus who misinform us that there is no God. In this, too, Nietzsche was prophetic.

64. Ibid. p. 236 (*GS* 285, pp. 229–30).

65. Pt. 2, "On Human Prudence," in *VPN*, p. 256. The attraction of evil for Nietzsche is the attraction of the power it promises.

66. *VPN*, pp. 570–71.

67. The Purified Self is a portal for God; in fact, it is the Superman in the Sufi sense.

68. We are at the doorstep of biotechnology, where even greater dangers lie in wait. All we need to claim godhood is to create life; even worse, a human being—Frankenstein all over again.

69. Quoted in Arthur Koestler, *The Sleepwalkers,* Harmondsworth, England: Pelican Books, 1968 [1959], p. 153.

70. Of course, it was wartime, and people were afraid Hitler might get the Bomb first. But what of its actual use? At the Nuremberg trials, the Nazi war criminals used exactly the same argument: "It was wartime, and we were under orders." It is a thorny ethical problem that cannot be resolved on an individual but only on a social basis. The solution is to have a society in which a Hitler cannot appear, and in which those in command do not make ethically unjustified use of weapons as a result of the moral debility of society. But this can be accomplished only by widespread instruction in a proper religion.

71. Indeed, in any society and civilization.

72. Quoted in Edward J. Larson and Larry Witham, "Scientists and Religion in America," *Scientific American*, September 1999, p. 83.

73. Frank Miele, "Darwin's Dangerous Disciple: An Interview with Richard Dawkins," *Skeptic* Vol. 3, No. 4, 1995, pp. 80–85.

74. Quoted in David Berlinsky, "The Deniable Darwin," *Commentary,* Vol. 101, No. 6, June 1996.

75. See e.g. *ibid.* (don't miss the hilarious fictional encounter with Borges!), and the debate with readers in the September 1996 issue.

76. Quoted in Arthur Koestler, *Bricks to Babel,* London: Picador, 1980, pp. 417–18.

77. In this connection, see also biologist John Cairns' discovery of "directed mutation"—J. Cairns *et al., Nature, 335* (1988) 142–45, and the ensuing debate.

78. From Mehmet Akif Ersoy, *Safahat* ("Stages").

79. Zbigniew Brzezinski, *Out of Control,* New York: Simon & Schuster, 1995. Available online at http://www.mcad.edu/classrooms/POLITPROP/palace/library/ou tofcontrol2.html (accessed July 8, 1998).

80. "Ordnung im Chaos," *Spiegel,* April 3, 2000, www.spiegel.de/spiegel/nf/0,1518,71442,00.html (accessed May 13, 2000).

81. At least 35 million, according to *The Economist* (Survey: 20th Century, "The Last Emperors," September 11–17, 1999). The lesson should not be lost on us that Communist Russia and China were both atheistic states, which thus unleashed the ego. Together with Nazi Germany, furthermore, they represented societies in which one man, instead of God, was idolized.

82. If man is regarded as a soulless lump of clay, it then becomes permissible to inflict one's will on him. Combined with the Base Self's drive to play God, the denial of a God-given inviolable spirit in man becomes a step to the egotistical self's proving that it is "god" over that helpless lump of clay.

83. George Steiner, *In Bluebeard's Castle,* New Haven: Yale University Press, 1971, pp. 54–55.

84. *GS,* Section 346, p. 287.

85. Quoted in Heller, pp. 168–69.

86. Not as a mental construct or thought or imagination or projection, but as man's very essence.

87. *VPN,* Section 60, p. 652.

88. See Jung, Vol. 1, p. 233n13.

89. The word "evil" is generally used in the sense of "ill" in this book.

90. "What is good? Everything that heightens the feeling of power in man, the will to power, power itself.
"What is bad? Everything that is born of weakness." *VPN* p. 570 (*Antichrist* 2).
For comparison, one might attempt to define the Islamic concept of Good as follows: "anything that furthers the *material and spiritual* well-being of Man." The opposite of this would be Bad.

91. Ibid. p. 343.

92. The "Alpa" cried out three times by the dreamer may be a coinage based on *Alp,* the old High German word for nightmare. Or it may be the personified bringer of the nightmare, the demon

who sits on the dreamer's chest causing evil dreams. This part of the dream is biographical: in the summer of 1877, Nietzsche related that in a dream he had to climb an endless mountain path; just below the mountain peak, he came across a cave. Out of its dark depths, a voice called out to him: "Alpa, Alpa—who is carrying his ashes to the mountain?" (quoted in Lampert, p. 333n82). Thus Zarathustra's dream might be a composite.

93. *VPN*, pp. 246–47 (*Thus Spoke Zarathustra*, Pt. 2: "The Soothsayer").

94. Jung, pp. 1226–29.

95. It is the same gate, with his intellect on the one side and his unconscious on the other.

96. For the sake of those in dire need of help—invocation of the sacred name: "Allah."

97. Quoted in Lampert, p. 38 (*Ecce Homo*, "Books," 5).

2. THE UNIVERSE, ENLIGHTENMENT, AND ETHICS

98. Whitley Streiber, the author of *Communion*, once asked if the innermost and outermost edges of the universe meet. Not only do they meet, but they are actually One.

99. How does this happen? By way of suggestion, I would like to draw attention to the Tarski-Banach conjecture in mathematics, also known as the "Banach-Tarski paradoxical decomposition," whereby a ball or sphere can be subdivided and reassembled into a sphere of different size. This is a solely mathematical procedure that defies visualization or any easy comprehension.

100. "He [Ultimate Reality] is the spirit of the universe and its

administrator. Hence, the cosmos is a big man." Ibn Arabi, *Fusus al-Hikam*. (Because God made man in His own image.)

101. I have intentionally avoided using the term "superman" here, since Nietzsche has contaminated this word by associating it with Godlessness. The Perfect Man is the epitome of Godliness, not its opposite.

102. "Notes on the Twentieth Century," *Atlantic Monthly*, September 1997, pp. 90–100.

103. In what follows, we shall rely on descriptions underlying the great Sufi sage Ibn Arabi's *Fusus al-Hikam* ("Bezels of Wisdom" or "Wisdom of the Prophets").

104. These may also be called Eternal Archetypes, Divine Truths or Knowledge Forms—i.e., forms established in God's infinite Knowledge. These are the forms of Divine Attributes.

105. It should not be supposed that we are indulging in unprovable speculation. Just as more mundane quantities and information are based on the empirical observations of astronomers and astrophysicists, the information presented here is based on the empirical observations of Sufis. It involves the profoundest experiential states, and has nothing to do with metaphysical speculation.

106. Let me briefly explain what *majzub* means. If a person receives premature Unveiling in his quest for God, he will enter a limbo state where he is not "all there." His name indicates that he has been overwhelmed by Divine Attraction (*jazba*). In other words, he will eat and drink, come and go in this world, but the reality he is experiencing is not the consensus reality that we all share. He is partly here and partly "there." Our psychiatrists would fail to notice this distinction, and would probably

classify him as harmlessly insane. Such persons are given leeway and respected in the Middle East. Needless to say, not all madmen are *majzubs*.

107. This should not be misread as an endorsement of solipsism, whether individual or collective.

108. The ordinary, exoteric interpretation is that the verse refers to Adam. This is the esoteric meaning.

109. This is for the Babylonian Talmud. For the Jerusalem Talmud, the reference is: Tractate Sanhedrin, *Seder: Nezikin* (Order: Damages), 4, 5.

110. Not to be confused with Gnosticism, an early Christian sect.

111. Also remarked long before by luminaries such as John Muir, Thoreau, and others, as well as the Native Americans.

112. Barry Commoner, *The Closing Circle,* New York: Knopf, 1971.

113. "What's more, entanglement does not only apply to pairs of particles. . . . [I]n the typical quantum state occupied by any group of particles the links between the particles are mostly of a nonlocal character. Quantum theory isn't just a tiny bit nonlocal. It's overwhelmingly nonlocal. Nonlocality is the rule for our Universe." Mark Buchanan in *New Scientist,* 22 August 1998.

114. H.B.M. Dervish, *Journeys With A Sufi Master,* London: Octagon Press, 1987 [1982], p. 83.

115. A custom in the Middle East.

116. And sometimes to Rumi, but that is spurious.

117. The Torah of Moses, the Psalms of David, the Gospel of Jesus, and the Koran of Mohammed. What Yunus means is that the Golden Rule is the essence of all religions.

118. William C. Chittick, *Imaginal Worlds,* New York: State University of New York Press, 1994, p. 109.

119. In fact, I owe its inspiration to Bahauddin Naqshband, who said: "My enlightenment is similar to standing a needle on its end."

120. Note that man still can, and does, perform evil. This is an admonition, not a curtailment of the freedom of man. Yet we would like to do away with even this admonition.

3. SUFI PSYCHOLOGY: AN INTRODUCTION

121. A. Geylani, *Fethur Rabbani: Abdulkadir Geylani'nin Sohbetleri* ("Conversations," Ar.-Turk. tr. Yaman Arikan), Istanbul: Uyanish, 1985, pp. 147, 294–97, 461.

122. The boundaries of this sphere are defined by the $t = 0$ instant of the universe, which yields a radius of about 15 billion light-years.

123. For an in-depth treatment of the topics dealt with in this section, and to see how yesterday's science fiction becomes the cyberculture of today and tomorrow, see Mark Dery, *Escape Velocity,* New York: Grove Press, 1996.

124. Laurence Lampert, *Nietzsche's Teaching: An Interpretation of* Thus Spake Zarathustra, New Haven: Yale University Press, 1986, p. 263.

125. Ibid., p. 266.

4. THE WAY OF THE SELF

126. Famous Islamic scholar, twelfth century A.D. What he means is the Base Self, frequently referred to as "the self" for short.

127. In this chapter I have mainly followed the description given in Ibrahim Hakki Erzurumi, *Marifetname* ("Book of Gnosis"), Istanbul: Elif Ofset, 1980, Chapter 29.

5. THE WAY OF THE SPIRIT

128. Henry Corbin, *Spiritual Body and Celestial Earth,* Nancy Pearson (tr.), Bollingen Series XCI:2, Princeton, NJ: Princeton University Press, 1977 [1960], p. 294n24 and later writings.

129. Since such classifications show variations, the following outline is intended to be representative and suggestive, not definitive.

6. THE ESSENTIALS OF SUFI PRACTICE

130. A. Guillaume, *Islam,* Harmondsworth: Penguin, 1979 [1954], p. 68.

131. Phil Parshall, *The Cross and the Crescent* (1989), p. 70, paraphrased in Kate Zebiri, *Muslims and Christians Face to Face,* Oxford: Oneworld, 1997, p. 103.

132. Mircea Eliade, *Yoga: Immortality and Freedom,* Willard Trask (tr.), Princeton: Princeton University Press (Bollingen Series), 1971 [1954], p. 135.

133. Material energies, such as cosmic rays, are not meant here.

134. Eliade, pp. 48–49.

135. Eliade, p. 216.

136. Ernest Wood, *Yoga,* Harmondsworth: Penguin, 1968 [1959], p. 200.

137. Peter Kelder, *Tibetan Secrets of Youth and Vitality,* Wellingborough, England: Aquarian Press, 1988. See the section on the Sixth Ritual.

138. Selvarajan Yesudian and Elisabeth Haich, *Yoga and Health,* London: Unwin Books, 1969 [1953], p. 122.

139. Shaykh al-Alawi, *Knowledge of God,* Norwich: Diwan Press, 1981, pp. 299–300.

140. This method of breath retention is practiced among the Sufis and is not generally known among Moslems.

141. Since the original of the Koran is in Arabic, recitations are normally in this language. However, those who find this too difficult can recite prayers in their own language, or in any other— God understands all languages. Nonetheless, we always say that something is lost in translation, and this is especially true in the case of the Koran. Hence, reciting prayers in Arabic is advisable for maximum effect.

142. Shaykh al-Alawi, pp. 79–166.

7. *THE SATANIC VERSES* AND THE DEMOCRATIC PERSONALITY

143. Salman Rushdie, *The Satanic Verses,* New York: Viking, 1988, pp. 208, 210–11, 212, 214–15.

144. Eric Rouleau, "Islam confronts Islam in Iran," *Le Monde*

Diplomatique (English edition), June 1999.

145. Bernard Lewis, "Islam and Liberal Democracy: A Historical Overview," *Journal of Democracy*, Vol. 7, No. 2 (1996), p. 62 (http://www.mtholyoke.edu/acad/intrel/blewis.htm).

146. Rushdie, pp. 210–11.

147. Bernard Lewis, op. cit., pp. 52–63 (http://www.mtholyoke.edu/acad/intrel/blewis.htm). For more details, see Bernard Lewis, *The Political Language of Islam*, Chicago: University of Chicago Press, 1988.

148. Robert A. Dahl, *Democracy and Its Critics*, New Haven: Yale University Press, 1989, pp. 14–15.

149. This is a rich term, other meanings being "City of Virtue" and "the Good Civilization."

150. Richard Walzer, *Al-Farabi on the Perfect State*, Oxford: Clarendon Press, 1985, pp. 229–31.

151. Farabi in *al-Siyasa al-Madaniyya*, quoted in Walzer, p. 454.

152. Thomas Metzger, "The Western Concept of the Civil Society . . ." www-hoover.stanford.edu/publications/he/21/b.html (accessed November 3, 1999).

153. Dahl, pp. 85–86.

154. George Soros, "The Capitalist Threat," *The Atlantic Monthly*, February 1997, pp. 45–58. (See also his follow-up in "Toward a Global Open Society," *The Atlantic Monthly*, January

1998, pp. 20–32.)

155. Ibid.

156. United Nations Human Development Report, 1998, as reported in the *New York Times,* September 28, 1998.

157. *Forbes* Magazine, "The Forbes 400," www.forbes.com (accessed September 25, 1999).

158. "The Seer of Silicon Valley Strikes Again," *U.S. News,* October 25, 1999.

159. *UN Human Development Report,* 1998.

160. "Occult Persons, Paid Failure," *Der Spiegel,* 8 November 1999.

8. THE STATION BEYOND ALL STATIONS

161. More precisely, his space is Nonspace (*la-maqaan*).

162. What it is called in Christianity is left as an exercise for the reader.

163. Richard Wilhelm (tr.), *The Secret of the Golden Flower,* New York: Harcourt, Brace & World (Harvest), 1962, p. 129.

164. John 3:3. "Born again" also means "born from above" in the original Greek. The Grand Sage uses "the Angelic World" (*malakut*) in place of "Kingdom of God."

165. I.e., the seeds of the male and the female. The Grand Sage is here actually providing an explanation of the most secret teachings of Jesus, the keys to which are to be found in the Koran. From Geylani, *The Mystery of Mysteries.*

166. Beautiful handmaidens.

167. A reference to "Die before you die."

168. *Futuhat* II, 133.19; quoted in William Chittick, *Imaginal Worlds,* New York: State University of New York Press, 1994, p. 63.

169. Ibid., p. 64.

170. "Withersoever you turn, there is the face of God" (2:115). We have already seen that pantheism, or collapsing God onto the universe, is not an option. Our poets are singing of the Vision of Unity, as opposed to the Vision of Multiplicity. And as soon as we are in the latter frame of reference, we have to acknowledge that God is distinct from—above and beyond—the universe: He is its Creator, while it is creation.

171. Such mystical utterances do not annul the reality of multiplicity we experience in everyday life. They are, strictly speaking, incorrect to the extent that they use the terminology of multiplicity for phenomena pertaining to the domain of Unity, where there could be no "I," "you" or "he," and nothing whatever could be said, all language being based on distinctions. In the realm of Unity, language breaks down, which is why "Those who know do not talk, those who talk do not know" (a saying of the Sufis that is also echoed in the *Tao Te Ching*). To the extent that "you" and "I" can be spoken of, their predicates continue to exist. Such utterances, therefore, reflect an impression born of extreme proximity. Hallaj expresses this beautifully:
You bring yourself so close to me,
I come to think that You are me.
        —Hallaj (*Diwan*).

APPENDIX

172. "The Taliban: Exporting Extremism," *Foreign Affairs*, November 1999.

173. See e.g. William T. Vollmann, "Across the Divide," *The New Yorker*, May 15, 2000, pp. 58–73; Jeffrey Goldberg, "The Education of a Holy Warrior," *The New York Times Magazine*, June 25, 2000.

174. "Talibinization of Pakistan's Transitional Democracy," *World Affairs*, Sept./Oct. 1999.

175. "A Chance for Peace in Afghanistan," *Foreign Affairs*, January/February 2000.

176. "'Tribal' Acts Giving a False View of Muslims," *Irish Times*, October 1, 1997.

INDEX

Y

Z